Contents

DISASTER PROOF YOUR CAREER

TACTICS TO SURVIVE, THRIVE AND KEEP AHEAD IN THE WORKPLACE

PATRICK FORSYTH

Kogan Page

LONDON PHILADELPHIA NEW DELHI

Publisher's note

Every possible effort has been made to ensure that the information contained in this book is accurate at the time of going to press, and the publishers and author cannot accept responsibility for any errors or omissions, however caused. No responsibility for loss or damage occasioned to any person acting, or refraining from action, as a result of the material in this publication can be accepted by the editor, the publisher or the author.

First published in Great Britain and the United States in 2010 by Kogan Page Limited

120 Pentonville Road	525 South 4th Street, #241	4737/23 Ansari Road
London N1 9JN	Philadelphia PA 19147	Daryaganj
United Kingdom	USA	New Delhi 110002
www.koganpage.com		India

© Patrick Forsyth, 2010

The right of Patrick Forsyth to be identified as the author of this work has been asserted by him in accordance with the Copyright, Designs and Patents Act 1988.

ISBN 978 0 7494 5954 3
E-ISBN 978 0 7494 5955 0

British Library Cataloguing-in-Publication Data

A CIP record for this book is available from the British Library.

Library of Congress Cataloging-in-Publication Data

Forsyth, Patrick.
  Disaster-proof your career : tactics to survive, thrive and keep ahead in the workplace / Patrick Forsyth.
      p. cm.
  ISBN 978-0-7494-5954-3 -- ISBN 978-0-7494-5955-0 (ebk) 1. Career development. 2. Vocational guidance. I. Title.
  HF5381.F6824 2010
  650.1--dc22
                                        2009040340

Typeset by Saxon Graphics Ltd, Derby
Printed and bound in India by Replika Press Pvt Ltd

Preface

Success doesn't come to you, you go to it.
— Marva Calins

Whatever job you may do the maxim quoted above is not a bad one to adopt. The world does not owe you a living. Nor these days can you realistically assume that regular, automatic assistance will be forthcoming from an organization (if one such employs you) intent on doing everything possible to further your career, or even to assist you satisfactorily perform the job you do for them currently. You need to take the initiative and adopt an active approach to developing your competence to do what you need to be able to do now, and what you want to be able to do in the future. This book, or rather the approaches it advocates, is designed to help you:

- become secure in your existing job and role;

- be ready and able to take on new challenges;

- appear an asset to your organization (and your boss) making you worth developing and promoting on up and through the organization structure;

- be desirable in the job market if you choose to move on to another employer;

■ obtain fair and satisfactory rewards for what you do (and improve this too, if that is an aim).

To a degree, the need for this is true of every job; everyone needs to be what we might call 'career fit'. Certainly this book addresses anyone working in an organizational environment regardless of age, seniority, gender or experience and whatever type of industry or kind of organization they work in. The situations it addresses are widely true across the globe also.

Its message is addressed to the individual rather than the organization or employer. It makes reference to the organization, of course, but the focus is on the individual and on individual action: on you and what you can do. It looks at how to make what you do and how you do it successful; and at how to make it go on being successful over time.

Change is the norm

Why is this so important? It is not just because of the competitive nature of the modern work environment, but also because every aspect of the workplace can get more volatile following any particular economic upheaval. Let us be clear about this right at the start: change is the norm. We can expect change to continue and for the pace of change to continue to increase. As Steve Case, Chairman, AOL Time Warner once said, 'There will be more confusion in the business world in the next decade than in any decade in history. And the current pace of change will only accelerate.' This comment will remain relevant for a good while and such a situation affects everything that follows here.

Change may seem a fairly benign word, but it can be almost normal for disaster to stalk the land. Certain industries, such as banking, once seemed stable, but they are as subject to difficulties and staff lay-offs as any other sector. Whenever jobs are in jeopardy and when any kind of cull happens a choice is usually made. Management does not usually decide to lose the best people, and those who are performing poorly, thought less of or are simply more of an unknown quantity may quickly find themselves in the firing line.

This book is not designed to help if disaster strikes, but to make the chances of that happening to you less and, possible disaster apart, to help you excel in a secure, satisfying and rewarding career. It is certainly true also that being career fit will help you recover if disaster should strike.

The very nature of the modern organizational environment means that success is always to be laid primarily at your door; so too is failure. You have to get things right, and you may get no second chances. And this is as true of your career as it is of your job.

Whatever your expertise at present, it is a fact that its nature and level will need to change. This may mean major extension if you are a newcomer to your chosen field, or it may mean what is better described as fine-tuning – though this may still be of considerable significance and influence ultimate success very much. Whatever it may necessitate, you must ensure that you are always 'career-fit' now and at any time in the future.

So, you must ensure this change takes place. You must ensure that your knowledge is kept up to date, your expertise and skill continue to be finely tuned and that you are able to do an equally outstanding job tomorrow, next week or next year whatever new circumstances you face.

The book reviews how you can achieve just that. It looks at an aspect of what might be called active career management, at what makes the process manageable, and what makes it effective. For the employee wanting to become – or remain – successful, inaction is simply not an option. Perhaps we might wish otherwise, but as Beverly Sills said: *There are no shortcuts to any place worth going.*

> **!**   **ACTION:** To get the best from reading this book it is worth keeping pen and paper close at hand, noting when anything mentioned seems to have direct application for you and specifying specific action you will take (even if this is simply to consider something further).

Hitch your wagon to a star; keep your nose to the grindstone; put your shoulder to the wheel; keep an ear to the ground; and watch the writing on the wall.

— Herbert Prochnow

1

The 21st-century workplace

The business world is an extension of the kindergarten sand box – but with quick sand.
— Richard F Stiegele

Unless you have the luxury of not having to work, your work is likely to be a major part of your life. Most people want two things from this: rewards (essentially financial reward) and job satisfaction. If you are going to spend a major part of your life working, then it is surely best to do something you like. Remember what the journalist Katherine Whitehorn said: 'The best career advice to give the young is: find out what you like doing and get someone to pay you for doing it' – perhaps good advice at any age. This is important in terms of the work you choose or, realistically, as sometimes happens, that you fall into, and also in working to ensure that you maximize the job satisfaction and rewards you get from whatever you do.

We do not choose or undertake our work in a vacuum, of course. Decisions need to be made in context of the broader world. And this broader world of work has changed radically in the last decade. As the 21st century moves on any individual is right to wonder how their career will progress and whether it will give them what they want.

Yet uncertainty is the order of the day.

Many, certainly those with some years' experience, may feel they remember 'better times', that is times when there was more certainty about how a career would progress. Many organizations once had defined career paths for people and, although progress varied somewhat, once on a specific path the direction in which you would be able to go was reasonably clear. In some industries this was particularly so. Banks make a good example, yet banks have changed too, more than many kinds of organization and, many would say, not for the better. Now, though this kind of prescribed career path does still exist, it is less common.

Some people may hanker for a return to these 'better days', but waiting for things to return to 'normal' is simply not one of the options. There are currently few, if any, safe havens, and few, if any, organizations that seem likely to be so again in a situation where change is the norm. Organizations are always likely to be under pressure and the well-being of their employees is often a lesser goal than sheer survival. All sorts of factors contribute to there being a different workplace and work culture than that of the past, and include:

- organizations being under greater market and financial pressure;

- changes in the way business and organizations operate (think of the IT revolution or international pressures, for instance);

- lower staff numbers and more pressure on individuals;

- reduced budgets and thus a reduced ability to fund personal development;

- changed terms of employment (think of how the pension schemes offered have changed in the last few years);

- more competition between employees to succeed;

- higher unemployment;

- a general increase in both the amount and speed of change;

- the greater likelihood of employers having to take sudden and negative action to protect themselves (such as making people redundant – in case of real disaster you may need *The Redundancy Survival Guide* by Barry Cushway and Rebecca Corfield, 2010, Kogan Page).

Despite all this you no doubt want to thrive, prosper and get on; and you probably want to enjoy your job while you do so. And remember it is said that if success were easy, there would be no such thing as failure. So what is the moral? How can you ensure that you do well? The simple answer is that there is nothing you can do that will *guarantee* success (if there ever was). But there is a great deal you can do to make success more likely. And this is what this book is about.

The way ahead

Let us be clear: this is not a guide to how to apply for a new job successfully, though it touches on some of the issues. Nor is it a guide to *career planning and development* in the corporate sense; that is it is not about how a company may organize career paths for people, or at least for some people, though again this is mentioned.

Rather it is about *the career enhancement made possible by career management* in the sense of the analysis, planning and action that can be taken by an individual at any stage of their career – and ideally throughout it – to *actively* increase the chances of their doing well, by ensuring that they are in a state that actively makes success more likely. The concept of it being an *active* process is key. For the most part, success comes not to those who sit and wait, nor even to those who take advantages of opportunities as they may occur, though this should be part of it. Success has to be *actively* sought. In today's volatile and competitive world of work perhaps *very* actively sought puts it better. What is more, you have to have a clear idea of what you mean by 'success' to have any chance of moving purposely towards it. So, defining goals, financial and of every other sort, is inherent to the process.

For the successful careerist this means a number of things. You must adopt the right attitudes, study and analyse the area and circumstances in which you work, plan and implement action to assist in boosting your competence and thus your progress. You need to be quick on your feet, ready for anything so that you can adjust longer term plans tactically and fine-tune your actions as necessary.

Basic preparations and precautions

To be ready and able to progress in your career you need to have certain thinking done and certain actions taken. Some examples follow:

CVs: The curriculum vitae (CV) is a document everyone should have on file. Not only should you have one, you should keep it up to date. Make a note on your file copy about any events (particularly successes) that need adding and about anything that needs deleting or replacing with something more appropriate; then on a regular basis, perhaps a couple of times each year, rework it. Remember too that a CV is not a standard document. If you need to use it, to apply for a new job say, then you need to review it and tailor it appropriately, emphasizing those things that might appeal especially to a particular potential employer. The same applies to covering letters designed to accompany CVs.

Watch the job market: If you are at a stage where you have decided that moving on is the right way forward, then do so well informed. Of course, you want to watch for particular opportunities, an advertisement for the perfect job, say, but you want to do this as part of a wider scan, one that informs you about the state of the market, salary levels, where demand seems to exist and so on. There can be a danger of jumping at one good thing seen, only to find later that in broader terms it was not as good as it seemed. If you are more urgently seeking a new opportunity then you need to become active:

you may need to register with recruitment consultants and websites or get in touch with headhunters.

Watch and liaise internally, too: Promotion is often as much of an opportunity as a move and you need to take notice of your surroundings; network and generally be aware of changes, developments and possible opportunities – more on this as the book continues.

Personal rules: It is a good idea to make some *rules* for yourself in terms of the way you will conduct yourself. At a point where you are satisfied with your job, and trust the people with whom you work, this may seem unnecessary. However, you may come to bless the day you abide by such self-imposed rules. Include things such as:

- always get things in writing (this includes job offers, changes to job descriptions, promises about remuneration etc);

- never cut off your options until you have to do so;

- always question the reason even for good things (you need to understand what is going on and why);

- check regularly to ensure that you know how your situation compares (for example with your salary and remuneration package) – this may or may not prompt action, that is a matter of choice and circumstances;

- record and update your career management records on a regular basis.

Rules devised – stick to them.

The power of communications

Without communications there would be no work, no achievement and no organization. You probably spend much of your time communicating, and every time you do so you not only pass on a message, an instruction – whatever – you also *say something about yourself*. Together with the achievement of your work objectives this is perhaps the most important factor to influence your career. You might be surprised how much a short, powerful, well-described description can achieve. Avoid statements that begin with 'it's sort of ...' and aim to be memorable where it matters.

So, there are three overall areas to be approached carefully here:

1. *Communication skills:* few people are going to progress success-fully in their career unless effective communication is one of their strengths. It is necessary to the job you do and to the process of career management. You need to define those skills that matter to you. These might include: listening, persuading, being assertive, negotiating, questioning and more. You may have to be as good at communicating in writing (from a long report to a succinct e-mail), in a formal presentation, or in – or chairing – a meeting, as well as simply face to face. Once you know what is important, you need to find out what makes the techniques work and learn, and practice, so that you excel at them. Communication can be fraught with difficulty; but, make no mistake, do it well and you achieve more and stand out as someone to be reckoned with.

2. *Communication intentions:* one of the keys to success in commu-nicating is to be sure of your intentions – are you: instructing, explaining, prompting discussion, persuading; or several of these at one time? Adopt and follow clear objectives and things will go better.

3. *Link to your personal goals:* finally, your manner and style of communication must reflect your personal goals and give the impression you want. Do not overlook this (see 'creating the right personal profile' over the page).

People power

It is rightly said that who you know is as important as what you know. People are a significant part of your passport to a successful career. There are those who succeed by riding roughshod over others, but such an approach is inherently risky (you may rule it out on other grounds, too). In career terms it can lose you sympathy and make you enemies, and this in time can prevent your further progress.

Leave relationships with people in aid of getting the job done on one side for the moment. In career terms, people come in various categories. There are those who are, potentially or actually:

- *helpful* (actively or just in the sense of being a source of information or advice);

- *able to recommend or pass on information about you*;

- *competitive with you*;

- *against you* (for whatever reason);

- *allies* (in the sense that you work together);

- *mischievous* (perhaps they are rumour spreaders or seen in a light that makes them inappropriate for you to be seen as allied with);

- *irrelevant*: and thus not worth wasting time on (at least from a career point of view).

However you categorize people in this kind of way you need to actively work with or through people, so:

- Keep good people records (the day you want to check who it was you met at a conference in New York two years back, you should be able to turn up the details).

■   Network and keep in touch (remembering that networking is an active process and a two-way one; it is not just a matter of keeping in touch with those who can help you, it is a matter of being helpful to them). Allocate it some regular time.

■   Ensure that you have people in place for specific purposes. Who do you turn to when you need advice or assistance on some particular matter? Do you have a mentor(s)? We return to mentors later.

Your relationship with others is likely to be a fundamental factor in your success; never become so busy or self-centred that you lose touch with those you need to work with or keep tabs on.

Creating the right personal profile

Whatever your level of self-confidence is, and even if you may feel you are obviously destined for the top, you should work at presenting the right profile to the workplace and to the world. This is not a question of defrauding people and pretending to be something you are not – acting out a persona that is not really you. It is a question of making your strengths clear and perhaps making them more obvious. First you have to decide what sort of person you want to be seen as being. This needs some analysis. It is no good saying *I must be seen as a professional operator*. What does that mean?

You may decide it means you should be seen as: experienced, expert, a good communicator, good (and perhaps patient) with people, an innovator, creative, good with attention to detail, empathic, caring, sincere – and more. You decide; but the list must make sense in terms of what you do, what you want to do and the environment in which you work. Thus, two things are important here:

1. deciding the profile you want;

2. actively working at putting it over.

You need to consider how this occurs. For instance:

- *you and your manner:* everything from the way you make a presentation to how you conduct yourself at a meeting;

- *your appearance:* dress, tidiness and appropriate professionalism;

- *your things:* that is your desk, office, briefcase, even files you carry into a meeting; muddle here can be read as inherent inability in more serious areas;

- *your dealings with others:* from having time for people, to being helpful, supportive or more.

Literally everything contributes. For example, if you write well (or can learn to) and it is important that this skill is in evidence, then you may need to contrive projects that provide an opportunity to use this communication skill. If the impressive reports you create are then seen by those in a position to make decisions about other things that you might do in future, that may help you. It is a sensible question to put to yourself in many situations; not just can I do this? But, if I do it, and do it well, how will I appear? Everyday activities will allow you to consciously and progressively build a positive image.

Office politics

The office without office politics does not exist. As this has an effect on you, you need to understand it and get involved, and perhaps control it, in the right sort of way. The situation here is that there are those that see a side of working in an organization that has little to do with getting the work done. Work provides, after all, a social environment and it is unsurprising if people react to that, but sometimes the effects are negative. Rumours are one example. There is apparently nothing that some people like more than feeding the rumour mill. So, with an eye on your profile and career you should:

■ Understand what goes on. If you remain aloof and detached from it all you may both miss opportunities and, worse, miss problems – or attacks; let us not forget that corporate life is competitive – that may adversely affect you.

■ Use the situation appropriately. You should probably not join the rumour-mongers, and certainly not be seen as a rumour starter, but you should, for example, be plugged into the grapevine or again you may miss out.

This area can be a minefield. Care is essential in terms of both what you do and what is, or may be, done to you. If you stay ahead of the game you can act accordingly, and in time. Remember the graffiti that said – *It is difficult to see the writing on the wall, when your back's to it.*

Achievement and results

There is only one, but strong, message to bear in mind here. It is a truism that *you should never confuse activity with achievement.* For the most part, the opportunities in corporate life come largely from achieving what is required of you. Looking busy, being busy, having difficulties, succeeding with peripheral matters with which no one else seems to bother, none of these are as important as meeting your main objectives.

So, perhaps the most important rule for the careerist is this: successfully achieving your goals or targets (whatever form they take) is of first importance in building your career, *indeed it is the foundation of everything else you do.* Attention to this is a prerequisite and although many other matters, as we have seen, need attention as part of career management, the effectiveness of all of them is reduced, perhaps drastically reduced, by any failure of achievement. *Note:* beware, it is a dangerous trap to feel that provided you are achieving successfully all is well and no further action is necessary. Even competent people can be overlooked and real shrinking violets are in most danger of this – at worst, look like a doormat and people will tend to walk all over you.

Perhaps this leads to one more useful principle – timing. The best moments to press home and initiate action to further your career may be when things are going well. Going to your manager for a raise just after some project has overrun its deadline and incurred costs double its budget, may not be too clever.

A management role

Perhaps you currently manage others, perhaps not. Although it is not suggested that the only way to be successful is to manage other people, there are things about management that are worth noting. In organizations many, perhaps most, of the senior jobs involve management. This fact reflects the way organizations are, and it links to the hierarchical nature of organizations, too. Of course, there are specialist positions that do not involve this whose incumbents are, by any measure, successful. But management is a prime route to success in most organizations. Furthermore, when management is added to someone's responsibilities it almost always adds to their rewards.

That said, management is not for everyone, nor is it something that everyone can do well. But if you can do it, or become able to do it, (and you might just find it very satisfying) then it is something to consider. If you reject the management route, you reject a good many options and rule out success being achieved in one of the classic ways.

Management is a broad discipline, and it is beyond the brief to review the many techniques that make it successful here (though there are other books that can help you do this). However, it does make a good example of the need to link the realities of organizational life to your own plans. Maybe this is something you have to be able to do to get to where you want. Maybe you can bypass it – or perhaps it is already something you want to do.

Note: while on the subject of management, your own manager is key (more of this later), but it should be recognized that some managers are bad, and a few so bad that career progress while reporting to them is unlikely and the immediate aim must be to change that.

Constant readiness

The possibility to advance your career can arrive unexpectedly. It is a sensible watchword to be prepared to move quickly. Consider the following circumstances:

- *Internal opportunity:* an opportunity may occur unexpectedly: for example, a new project gives you the chance to apply for a step up and a new challenge, or an offer is made out of the blue.

- *Internal difficulties:* something changes that makes an urgent move suddenly desirable; say the section for which you work is to be reduced and will no longer be a helpful stepping stone along your chosen road.

- *Disaster strikes:* maybe the company is taken over and you are made redundant.

- *An external opportunity appears:* you have not planned to move on, but you see a job advertised, or are approached about one, that is too good an opportunity to miss.

When circumstances such as these occur, you may need to move fast. Hence the necessity to:

- keep your plan and thoughts up to date;

- have your CV regularly updated and ready for use (though you will doubtless need to edit it to a degree to match individual use);

- be able to find and document any record of achievement, from formal appraisals to letters of congratulation that might assist action;

- maintain relationships with any people useful to your career (eg who might offer a reference, advice or a job).

There are tasks to do regularly if this is to be the case, but it is annoying to find yourself delaying what should be prompt action because of simple updates not carried out.

New directions

Career progress may take you up an organization, around it (for example to another division or an overseas office), but ultimately – unless you are one of those now rare individuals who spend a lifetime with one employer – you will move on.

You need to be ready for this, too. One example makes a powerful point. Someone who is successful and works uninterrupted in an organization for a few years becomes distanced from the job-hunting process. If you have not attended a selections interview for a while, ask yourself – how would I do in one tomorrow?

You need to keep up to date in this regard too, with:

- *Skills:* how are your interview and allied skills such as listening and questioning?

- *HR practice:* what is expected of, and judged by, application forms, covering letters and CVs and what style and form suits best?

- *Examples:* if asked for details of work done, achievements or successes can you readily find appropriate examples to quote and speak about them in the right sort of way?

- *Tests:* have you studied how best to react to and conduct yourself with regard to psychometric and other tests you may be given as part of recruitment procedures? (How to succeed in psychometric tests is something else you may need to bone up on).

If – when – such opportunities come, maybe as a result of ground-work you yourself have done, you do not want them to go by default. Being prepared, on a broad front, is very much part of successful career management.

Going it alone: One final possibility for advancement and change should be noted. You may want, as an increasing number of people seem to do, to become your own boss. Whether this means working solo on a freelance basis or starting your own organization and employing others, it needs careful consideration.

Key is the fact that, however skilful you are in your own special area (maybe you are a designer of some sort and want to start a design company), you need a whole battery of skills to run your own show. Even a freelance must not just excel in the business concerned, they may need to understand marketing, certainly they must have some financial acumen, and also be sufficiently well organized to operate productively. Some, like me, rate this as the best decision they ever made, but it is not one to make lightly.

> **!**   **ACTION:** The factors described above are likely to be important to everyone. Working in a specialist field – or the characteristics of your own job – may make it sensible to think about other relevant topics in the kinds of way in which the above are approached here. This is an area in which making some notes may be useful.

Realistically career management is as much an art as a science. It is also, as has been said, a process that must be applied personally. You need to get to grips with what is appropriate for you, in your kind of job and with your hopes in mind. Certainly the process:

- demands clear thinking and analysis to put you on the right track;

- benefits from a systematic, and ongoing, approach;

- needs attention to detail to make it work;

- must be based on a sensitive reading of situations and people around you;

- necessitates good and considered decision making along the way;

- can be enhanced if you are quick on your feet and ready to take advantage of opportunities as they occur.

A final thought: never overlook the process, put it on one side or delay doing things that you know demand attention now. One way to look at it is as creating a situation in which you are *always* in the best possible position to be promoted or appointed to something new. Your attitude to career management, and the action you take as a result, can directly change your life and career – and do so for the better.

So, you need to have the management of your career in mind constantly. There will rarely, if ever, be stages where you can rest on your laurels, and while it must not distract you from doing a good job – this is, after all, one of the things that assist the achievement of success – action that affects your career must become a regular part of your thinking. Your career is affected by everything you do – and by everything and everyone around you. The world and other people around you are not necessarily all on your side. The stage on which your career is acted out is a competitive arena, and a constructive attitude is necessary therefore to combat possible difficulties along your career path as well as to do the positive things that will take you forward.

While there are more chrysalises than butterflies, flying free is worth the effort.

2

The Confidence to Succeed

If you think you can, you can
and if you think you can't, you're right.
— Mary Kay Ash

A fundamental basic to creating career success is belief and thus confidence. Ken Blanchard and Spencer Johnson, who together wrote the well-known book *The One Minute Manager*, are credited with saying, 'Everyone is a potential winner. Some people are disguised as losers, don't let their appearances fool you'. You need to be not only clear what you want to do, but also have confidence that you can do it, precisely so that you do not allow yourself to be disguised as a loser. Your career is an area in which to set your sights high; indeed I would go so far as to say that the danger of not doing so, and thus failing to achieve things you might otherwise do, is greater than the risk of setting your sights too high and not quite making the summit.

Say you work for a commercial organization. Do you want to be head of department or on the Board? Do you believe that you really can be one day? Or do you see this as a step too far? If it is the latter then it is easy not to take action that might take you there. But if you believe it is possible, recognize that it will take some effort and that there are steps along the way, then in fact you are taking the first step to getting there. Substitute what you want: becoming a manager, being posted to the Singapore office, being included in the profit-sharing scheme – the principle is the same.

Practical confidence building

So, the moral is simple, being confident is going to help you. But many of us cannot become instantly confident by just snapping our fingers and shouting *No problem!* It is easier said than done. Generating confidence needs working at; maintaining, too.

Some confidence comes with time and experience. Having found that you must do things that worry you to start with, yet that you survive and perhaps do them not just in a workmanlike fashion, but really well, gives you confidence as you face subsequent challenges. Even after only a dozen pages, I am confident that I can write this book, producing the requisite number of words and a useful message. That it is not to say that doing so is effortless (certainly I would hate my publisher to think that). It must be researched, planned, drafted and finalized. Nor, I think, is it arrogant. But I have written other books, I know the process and have learnt from previous projects, and it is this that gives me confidence. I can literally tick off numbers of things – tasks – and know that, although they may well require thought and care, I can do them and that a completed book will be the result.

If confidence can act as a secure foundation to your plans and activities, let's consider it brick by brick as it were. Overall, two things seem to me to instil and enhance confidence.

Understanding and dealing with negative self-talk

Psychologists use the word 'self-talk' to describe our instinctive feelings about things and it is common, faced with any uncertainty, for this to be negative. Think of the way an inexperienced presenter often feels prior to making a presentation. They think: it will be terrible, people will hate it, that they will lose their place, dry up and fail to get their message over; they worry, too, about a host of details from what to do with their hands to how to deal with questions. They feel the audience will be against them, that they lack the skills to project, gain attention and follow a logical structure and begin to hope profoundly that the ground will open up and swallow them before the introduction from the Chair is complete.

If someone feels like this, and sometimes it is difficult not to, then the chances increase that on the day it really will be a disaster. What's more, if it does go poorly, then the feelings are reinforced, and the next time things may seem and be even more difficult. What is the moral? Well, part of it is to recognize what is happening and reject this unwarranted self-talk. Here let me link to a second point.

Using knowledge to give you power

Lack of confidence often goes hand in hand with lack of knowledge. If you do not know something then a result can automatically be uncertain. Continuing with the example of making a presentation (because it is something most of us would concede benefits from confidence) consider some of the obvious fears.

Regularly in one aspect of my work, that of conducting courses to help people develop their presentation skills, I ask participants what factors they feel make them uneasy about presenting. *Everyone* has some fears, and the commonest stated usually include (in no particular order):

- butterflies in the stomach;

- a dry mouth making it difficult to speak;

- not knowing where to put your hands;

- fear of the reaction of the audience;

- fear of not having enough material;

- fear of not being able to get through the material in the time;

▪ not knowing how loud to pitch your voice;

▪ losing your place;

▪ over- or under-running on time;

▪ being asked questions you cannot answer;

▪ drying up.

All these main ones that seem to concern people are worth a specific comment and what deals with them best is a practical approach (that links to knowledge). There are actions that actually sort out, remove or reduce some of these problems, others are helped by the way you organize the speaking environment, and all can be regarded in a way that has a considerable effect on the presenter's ability to overcome any nerves.

What about the fears mentioned above?

▪ *Butterflies in the stomach:* this is a physical manifestation of any worries you may have. In mild form it does no harm and fades as the adrenalin starts to flow when you get under way. On the other hand a number of practical measures undoubtedly help reduce the feeling. Some are seemingly small, perhaps obvious; they do work, however, and may work better when some are used together. They include:

 – a few deep breaths just before you start;

 – no heavy food too soon before you start;

 – no starvation diets, or the butterflies will be accompanied by rumbles;

 – no alcohol (some would say very little) before the off.

▪ *Dry mouth:* again this is a natural reaction, but one simply cured. Just take a sip of water before you start. And never be afraid of asking for, or organizing, a supply of water in front of you. Place it where you are least likely to spill it and you may, like me, prefer to avoid the fashionably fizzy waters supplied by many of the venues where speakers often find themselves, especially hotels and conference centres. I am sure it is nice for the audience and offered with good intentions, but it is inclined to make you burp if you are the speaker. The longer the duration of your talk, the more you will need to take the occasional sip. Talking makes you dry and an air-conditioned venue or office compounds the problem. Act accordingly, throughout your talk.

■ *Somewhere to put your hands:* because somehow they can feel awkward. They seem like disproportionately large lumps at the end of your arms. The trick here is to avoid obvious awkwardness, give them something to do – hold a pen perhaps – and then *forget* about them (at least until they need to be involved in some gestures, but that's another issue).

■ *Audience reaction:* or rather the fear of a negative one. Ask yourself *why* they should react negatively. The fear may be irrational. It may be because you feel ill prepared – and preparation is certainly something that can boost confidence. And anyway remember that audiences hate poor presentations; they *want* you to succeed.

■ *Not having enough material:* this should simply not be a fear. Your preparation will mean you *know* you have not only enough but the right amount of material for the topic and the time.

■ *Having too much material:* this needs no separate comment from the previous point except that even if you start with too much, preparation should whittle it down to the appropriate amount.

■ *Not knowing how loud to speak:* this may be a reasonable fear in a strange room, but you can test it – ahead of the meeting find someone to stand at the back and check how you come over until you get the level right. In fact, a moment's thought shows that it is not really a very difficult problem. In other circumstances if a single person came into the room from a door at the far end, you would probably speak to them naturally at just the right level. Try not to worry and think of yourself as addressing the back row (though remember to switch off, I sometimes go home after a day conducting a course and am told, *Don't shout, you are not talking to the back row now*).

■　*Losing your place:* again there are practical measures to help, apart from knowing your message well, particularly in terms of the exact format of the speaker's notes that you opt to have in front of you; these can be designed specifically to reduce any likelihood of losing your place.

■　*Misjudging the timing:* judging the time (and finishing on time) is important. It can be difficult. In part, an accurate judgement of time comes with practice. But notes can flag regular checks, and of course, wear a watch with a clear dial and if necessary synchronize time with the Chairperson.

■　*Being asked questions you cannot answer:* no one is expected to be omniscient. Here let me say at once that it is not the end of the world to say: *I don't know* – always an important point for any would-be presenter to accept (though you might have to make some further comment, maybe, *I'll find out and get back to you*).

■　*Drying up:* here one must address the reason why this might happen. Dry mouth? Pause and have a sip of water, no one will mind. Indeed always do this if necessary, struggling on risks you ending up choking to a halt and having to pause much longer. Lost your place? If that does not happen you will not dry up, as your notes are organized to carry you forward. Just nerves? Well, some of the elements now mentioned – and preparation – will help. It is worth remembering here that time often seems to flow at a different rate for presenters and audiences. Often during presentation skills courses, where usually I am using video to record what participants do and prompting discussion about it, people will regularly criticize themselves about one perceived fault: *I dried up at one stage*, they say, *there was an awful great gap*. Yet no one noticed except them, and often when the video is replayed they cannot even spot where it happened. It just seemed too long to them at the time.

The same principle applies to the speaking environment: that's the room and particularly the immediate area you inhabit at the front of the room. For example, checking where the wires run when there is a projector or computer involved helps prevent you tripping over them. Incidentally, presentation skill is certainly something that many a career needs; I have written in detail on this in two books: *How to craft an effective business presentation* (Foulsham) and *The PowerPoint Detox* (Kogan Page).

Enough. But a detailed and clear example here is important and similar principles apply to many things. Your first appraisal will be easier if you have thought about it and use the knowledge you have about it to guide you. The meeting provides more knowledge and experience and the next one is less of a problem. In terms of attitude you should note that you need a practical approach to all these sorts of feelings. Just feeling *I'm worried,* is difficult to combat. But ask yourself *why* you are worried and you may well surprise yourself, discovering that there is a tangible reason for the fear, one that can be addressed by a practical solution that will remove or reduce whatever factor is creating the feeling and, at best, allow you to put it right out of your thoughts. With that principle in mind, consider not only a one-off event such as a presentation, but also the continuity of your career. Actively considering, monitoring and fine-tuning how it is proceeding gives you experience and knowledge and that assists you take a more confident approach to the next task.

You can learn and draw confidence from failure, too. Perhaps you ask for a rise in salary and this is rejected. Far from putting you off ever asking again, the feedback may well help you decide how and when to ask the next time and mean that when you do so you are more confident of the outcome.

It really does work to concentrate on the practicalities. Someone about to juggle with flaming torches may be confident that they will not burn holes in the carpet, but only because they have studied and are knowledgeable about the process (and have practised!).

> **!** **ACTION:** it may be useful to identify other areas about which you lack confidence, list those things that make you uncertain (as was done for making presentations above) and then see what practical remedies come to mind. This approach really does help.

Working to build confidence

Whatever approach you take, and there are many psychological approaches to building your confidence, such as visualizing your success (indeed some readers may feel such approaches are worth separate study), make no mistake, once confidence is built – it helps. I regularly come across evidence of this, especially with the participants I meet on training courses. Though some may swear by behavioural approaches, most people who display confidence seem to have a strong, practical element to their thinking about it.

Some examples

One example especially comes to mind: I was waiting in the reception area of a London radio station to be interviewed (something to do with small business, as I remember), and got into conversation with someone similarly waiting for their 'spot'. He was a technical guy and was to be interviewed about some environmental issue (pollution or some such, the details do not matter). I asked him if he ran the technical department in his organization, and I will always remember his reply: 'No', he said, 'but I will soon.' As we chatted he explained that he had spent time and effort cultivating the skill and opportunity to be the organization's spokesman on certain technical matters. This was done specifically to enhance his profile in the run-up to the current head of department retiring and the process of their replacement. He did well in his radio interview, and I would like to think that in due course he achieved the promotion he wanted.

Here, confidence was based on a combination of knowledge (of his technical and communications abilities), which inspired belief.

Believing he could succeed had led to a consideration of tactics (which otherwise might not have happened) and a good ploy being tried. His confidence and tactics seemed spot on to me. If we assume that he had likely done some research and thinking about the best way to come over on radio too, it makes an excellent example of an approach we can all usefully adopt, albeit in different circumstances.

This kind of thinking can link not only to strengths as above, but also to weaknesses. Another example: opening a public course on business writing I once asked for delegates to introduce themselves. One question I asked was simply 'Why are you here?' I will always remember one person's reply: 'I'm here because I'm missing out,' he said. Asked to explain, he said that he knew his manager was avoiding involving him in any project that required a report to be written at its conclusion because, as he put it: 'I write such a rotten report.' Report writing can be a chore, but well done it is certainly a career skill and reports, any written document for that matter, say a great deal about their writer (that is, beyond their content as people read between the lines as it were taking a message from the style and choice of words). His response was to get himself on a course, and quick.

Again this is an example of the right attitude and, I think, of confidence, too. He may have had no confidence in his current level of skill in this respect, but he was confident he could acquire the necessary skills and was determined to do so. He recognized the *opportunity* of developing a particular skill and acted to move towards it.

Many things can be usefully viewed this way. The opportunity is not simply to correct something; in this case to become able to write good reports. It is to move to excelling at anything that is both necessary to the current job and that helps cultivate a profile of competence. In this case he was well aware that although a course could help to set him on the right path, he would need to practise and go on thinking about it in order to get to where he wanted.

Towards future confidence

Perhaps the ultimate moral here is to cultivate the habit of being realistic about yourself and how you operate (warts and all), taking steps to move forward and thinking positive about the whole process. Remember the saying attributed to Anna Freud, *I was always looking outside myself for strength and confidence, but it comes from within. It is there all the time.*

Finally, let me add that you will tend to approach something better and find more confidence in doing so if you view the task in the right way. Perhaps a story helps make the point. An American college student is going on an exchange visit, swapping with a student from a small town in northern Thailand. After much planning and preparation, and with some apprehension, she sets off on the long journey. After a long international flight and a domestic flight, she is sitting in a car with her host travelling the final leg to the town where she will spend a year of her life.

She expresses her fears about the language, Thai being a notoriously difficult language to learn. Her host reassures her that she will manage it without difficulty but, unconvinced, she is totally disbelieving. 'It will surely not be difficult,' he repeats. Continuing, 'No one in your host family speaks English. You have no choice; you *will* learn to speak Thai.' (The full story is told in the book written by Karen Connelly, *Touch the Dragon*, Black Swan.)

Here it is not a question of whether the task is easy or difficult; it is simply necessary. If something is essential, many things can be achieved. Accepting that something is essential may be the first step to tackling it with confidence.

> **!** **ACTION:** Never let undefined fears cramp your performance; identifying and working at dealing with them really can remove some and reduce others and the net effect of such analysis is worthwhile.

3

Your Career Plan

*If you're not planning where you want to be,
what reason do you have for worrying about being
nowhere?*
— Tom Hopkins

If you are to influence your career, certainly if you are to positively
influence it, then you need to be clear about the direction in which
you want it to go. This may sound obvious and easy, but in fact
implies a good deal and needs some careful thought. When I was at
school I wanted to be an astronomer. This was born of a passionate
interest in the subject rather than any link with my actual or likely
abilities. Okay, this was way back when sex was safe and the
Russians were dangerous, and when the careers master at my school
was only really well able to discuss Latin verbs, but it was still my
earliest career plan. However, once I began to check out what might
be necessary, realism soon set in and, though my interest continues,
my career took other paths. Career planning, perhaps sadly, does
not mean just conjuring up plans that are no more than pie in the
sky, but must proceed on a clear, accurate and honest assessment of
what might be possible.

This must involve some inward analysis.

Self-assessment

We doubtless all like to think we know ourselves, but this may not be entirely true. It is easy to make assumptions, to leave key elements out of the picture and so, as a result, misjudge how our current profile lends itself to career progress, and just what sort of progress may be possible. Assumptions can link back to past experience, fears, bad experiences or a host of things. An example of just how much we may misjudge ourselves perhaps makes the point.

As a trainer, one of the things I do regularly is conduct courses designed to improve peoples' ability to make formal presentations. One category of person who attends (usually told to attend by their employer) has never done this, or done very little of it, hates the thought of it because they know they cannot do it well and would much prefer to avoid the whole subject and the task. Yet these same people, or certainly many of them, prove to be quick and effective at learning how to make a good job of a presentation. They find there is a difference between inherently not being able to do something and simply not knowing how to go about it. With the knowledge of how to tackle it, and with practice, an ability to make good presentations can be added to their list of skills. Yet previously they may have been avoiding tasks, jobs, even promotional opportunities, that were likely to put them in a position where they would have to do this seemingly worrying task.

There may well be aspects of your nature and ability that you think about in this way, so the first step to deciding a route forward from your current position is to look at where you are at the moment. This should be done systematically and honestly and you may find it useful to keep some notes of what the thinking produces. The next several sections lead you through a suitable and proven progression of self-analysis, which assesses your skills, work values, personal characteristics, and also your non-work characteristics.

Assess your skills

You might be surprised at how many skills you have. Remember that it is quite possible that things you do and take for granted, you can only in fact do because of considerable, and perhaps unusual, experience. So list all the things for which you have an aptitude. Some general headings under which to group your abilities may be:

- *communications:* everything from writing a report to issuing instructions;

- *influencing skills:* that includes persuading, negotiating and promoting ideas;

- *management:* everything to do with managing other people;

- *problem solving:* analysing and drawing conclusions and coming up with solutions;

- *creativity:* generating ideas, seeing things in the round, having an open mind;

- *social skills:* not just relating to people but having insight, helping others, facilitating;

- *numerical skills:* handling figures, statistics, accounts, etc and other numerical data;

- *special skills:* here such skills as speaking a foreign language, unusual technical skills, and so on should be mentioned;

- *computer literacy:* this is so much part of so many jobs these days, albeit to different levels, that it deserves its own heading.

Whatever stage of your career you are at, you should have the full picture in mind and recorded. Bear in mind too, that:

- such a list will change over time;

- you may see omissions in such a list; omissions that you resolve to fill in terms of adding or extending competencies.

Decide which headings along the lines of the above are right for you, and make some notes. It might be an interesting exercise to do this now, and again when you have read this whole book. Some of the topics listed above will reoccur as headings in their own right and you may view things differently after a review of how important some of the skill areas are from a career point of view.

Assess your work values

It is not enough to know what skills you have. These must be viewed alongside your work values. For instance, do you have:

- a strong need to achieve;

- a need for high financial reward;

- high work interest/satisfaction requirements;

- a liking for doing something 'worthwhile';

- a desire to do something creative;

- specific requirements (such as to travel, to be independent, innovative or part of a team)?

A wide range of permutations may be involved here and may change over time. For example, travel may be attractive to the young and single but less so to people who have young children, then it may become more attractive again when a family is older. Make notes here too.

Assess your personal characteristics

Most people do not change their habits and ways, at least they do not do so dramatically and certainly not without effort, once they are old enough to be into a career. You need to assess yourself in this respect and do so honestly. Are you innovative, positive, optimistic, hard working, prepared to take risks? What sort of a person, in fact, are you? There may be a clash here. In thinking through your work values you feel that you may be suited to, and want to be involved in, something with considerable cut and thrust, that is innovative, creative and which generally puts you working at the leading edge. However, an honest assessment of yourself may show that, whatever the superficial or status attraction of this option, it is just not really you. For example, risk taking may not be your thing and a different, perhaps more supportive role, may seem to be where you are likely to excel most. Again, list what you feel is relevant about yourself here.

Assess your non-work characteristics

Realistically, work and social life have to coexist alongside each other. They may do so peaceably, or there may be conflicts between them. It is not automatically necessary to career success to be a workaholic, though a strictly nine to five attitude to the job is perhaps not recommended (or possible) either. And on the positive side, work and interests or hobbies may overlap constructively, the one teaching you something about the other. There are questions to be asked here too:

- What are your family circumstances?

- Where do you need to live?

- How much time can you spend away from home?

- What are your other responsibilities and interests?

Consider family and interests specifically:

- **Family:** If you have a partner, wife or husband then priorities may need to be set, because career-building priorities can clash. It is, sadly, perfectly possible to arrive successfully at the top of the heap – a success in business, but with home, family and happiness in ruins. This may sound dramatic, but the issues here are worth some serious thought. Not least, there are times when career decisions must be made fast or opportunities will be lost. If the relationships between home, family and work have never been discussed, then the man who comes home from the office to tell his wife: 'I have this great new opportunity with the company, but it means living in Hong Kong for two years', is in for some heated debate, especially if he has promised to go back to the office the next day with a decision. Such situations can occur at every stage of a career. They are not dependent on which half of a partnership instigates them and are made more complicated when both partners work or if there is a dependent granny, children or... but you get the idea.

■   **Interests:** Interests are an important issue. All work and no play is, for most of us, a bad thing. You need to look at your interests and hobbies alongside the job and your future career intentions. Can they move forward together? How much time do you want to put into hobbies, social life and work? These are not easy questions and must be worked out over a period of time. Even so there may come times when there are clashes. If you have thought it all through, and discussed it with other family members as appropriate, then transient problems are more likely to be just that – transient.

■   **An international dimension:** this is worth a mention in its own right; indeed, you may want to engineer an international dimension to your work. In that case more detail appears in the boxed paragraph that follows; even if you do not, it may be worth a look as it provides a good example of the kind of thinking that can be helpful as you review specific possibilities.

A range of work opportunities

First, you may want to consider international opportunities as an element of your own career goals. The following may constitute major career moves; but they might also be undertaken on a temporary basis or as a minor part of your overall work portfolio for specific developmental advantage.

■   *Work for a multinational company:* if it suits you, then being in a multinational automatically extends the possibilities open to you. You have networking opportunities on a broader scale and may also have opportunities to relocate abroad in the future on some basis.

■ *Locate overseas:* a spell working overseas may demand some development to fit you for it. You may or may not see a spell in the Netherlands or New Zealand as a start of a lifetime there, or a lifetime in a variety of overseas locations, but you are certainly going to learn from it even in the short term. Myles Proudfoot, moved by Proctor & Gamble from the UK to corporate headquarters in Cincinnati says: 'The network of contacts I have developed and wide exposure to new people is helping me to connect with the latest ideas and opportunities… it has changed the way I see the business world, exposed me to new horizons and raised my expectations of what I want to do in the future.' He has had to adapt and adapt fast, but is learning a great deal, too. Already new responsibilities have involved him further in the international dimensions of the business and since then he has been located for a spell in both China and Belgium.

■ *Work in exporting:* this is a particular field of business, but it is one that normally gets you travelling and puts you in touch with people and organizations that may help your development plans. Although not for everyone, this is the kind of thing that well illustrates long-term development and progress. For example, if you may want to work abroad, a spell in export may be a step in the right direction. It may also be one that justifies language training, so that at some future date your learning and experience allow you to add 'Fluent in French and German' to your CV.

■ *Include an overseas travel element within your job:* all sorts of things might see you making trips abroad – and developing contacts and learning opportunities as you do so. Some things need nurturing. Can you be the company's representative on an international committee, nominated attendee at an exhibition or the person that briefs people at the overseas end of a new collaboration? My own work has involved a good deal of travel over the years, and I remember that the first time I ever went overseas was to a conference in France. For many years I have been, in part, what is called an invisible export. Over time I have learnt a great deal from acquiring something of an international perspective; this has helped directly with my work and added an enjoyable dimension to what I do. Even seemingly small things can be valuable. Once, for instance, attending an event in the States – the annual conference of the American Society of Training & Development – I was amazed at how much information and how many contacts could be accessed in just two days; a couple of further days exploring New Orleans where it was held that year was fun, too (before the hurricane damage).

A key element about all of this is people. Having a wide range of contacts is always likely to benefit your development, as you can learn so much from others, and ensuring some of them are overseas broadens the effect still more.

Remember that there are no right or wrong answers here and I would not presume to give prescriptive advice. The amount of time and energy a job needs to take up and what must be left for other things varies between individuals and rightly so; it would be a dull old world if we were all the same. The smooth planning of these issues certainly helps you make career decisions more easily and more promptly than would otherwise be the case. And for most people, success in life means career and private life working reasonably compatibly together, whatever the demands of the job at any particular moment. It may be worth listing characteristics alongside their compatibility with your job here as part of the overall analysis.

All this information forms the basis for much of the subsequent thinking that is then necessary as you consider how you may take action through the way you work and what you think and do so as to build your career successfully. Opportunities and your real circumstances constantly have to be compared. Some career paths will play to your strengths, others will not and some will cause a clash of objectives that will be problematical or will simply not be open to you because of your mix of talents and abilities (though this latter is something you can work at correcting). The picture you build up here, and your notes, are solely for *your own* benefit. Some of the facts and information may also be useful at appraisals and in the documentation and discussion that may be necessary if you wish to change employer. These are issues returned to later.

! **ACTION:** The assessment of your skills, work values, personal characteristics, no-work characteristics make a good start to a process of self-assessment. To make things manageable it makes sense to start with these (though there is more to come).

Obtain professional career guidance

Sometimes, the problem appears that as you try to analyse both yourself and the path you want to take, you can come to no real conclusion as to what will suit you best in the future. In this case, it may be worth seeking professional assistance. An example from my own circumstances may make a point clearer.

I came from a background that had no links with the commercial or business world. My father was a dentist and once he had got over the shock of my wanting to go into 'industry', insisted that I should first go to an organization (in London) called the Vocational Guidance Association. This body undertook to test the aptitudes of a person and match them to the type of job and career that seem most suited to the individual concerned. As my father was paying, I agreed to go, and found myself subjected to a battery of psychometric tests that lasted, as I recall, most of a day. I returned home and a report cataloguing what little ability I had at that stage arrived a few days later.

To cut a long story short, I did go into industry (initially into publishing and ultimately into marketing) and cannot now remember what difference, if any, the report made. What I do remember is finding the report many years later when I moved house. It described the nature of the job they had felt I would most enjoy, and I found it matched *exactly* those things with which I was involved at that time (having moved into consultancy and training). I have always had a greater respect for such services since. An objective view is sometimes useful, and although there is no test that will magically put you into a career where success will follow automatically because the match between you and what you are doing is so good that there is no other possible result, the prompt to your thinking that such analysis can provide may be very useful.

A range of such services are available in most large cities and they are by no means only designed for those moving from education to a first job (the time I did my tests) but can be useful at any stage of a career where you wish to check how your plan is progressing and whether you are going in a direction that is likely to produce job satisfaction. Choose a good advisor (by no means all those who offer career advice and testing are good) and this may, for some people, be a useful check at a particular stage of their career. Two last points are worth making:

- *Costs:* It may be worth saying here that there are things, like career counselling, that cost money and must be paid for by you. If it helps, so be it; certainly it is worth a thought – simply assuming that anything helpful will be paid for by an employer may see you losing out. Remember too, that even those employed and paying tax on their salary may be able to claim tax relief on certain developmental activities not covered by the employer. Here, where cost is an issue, any objective chat can help; the simplest version may be with a friend of colleague.

- *Records:* Notes made about organizations (such as career guidance advisors) are worth keeping. They may include a wide range of entities from websites and reference books and libraries to organizations and individuals who can help.

Finalizing your analysis

Linking your analysis of yourself with market demands

Whatever profile your various self-analysis exercises builds up, it must match realistically with the demands made by employers in the marketplace. Let me put that more specifically: it must match up with the demands made by employers in whatever sector you intend to excel in. So, although there are perhaps generally desirable characteristics that we might list: being adaptable to change (or able to prompt it), flexible, or thorough or productive and so on, there will be more specific characteristics in terms of abilities and nature that will be demanded in a particular field. Indeed, a certain competence or characteristic may be an asset in one area and frowned on in another, as something like creativity might be differently regarded in an advertising agency and a more traditional business. Similarly what for some is drive and initiative, might be regarded elsewhere as aggressive and self-seeking.

Two points arise from this. First, having analysed yourself and your intended field (even if you are already in it), you must aim to cultivate the appropriate profile for success in that field. Or, for some, to react to such analysis showing that you are *not* well suited in a way that encourages the possibility of success elsewhere. The better the match, the better the chances are that your profile will allow you to do well and progress along your chosen path.

Success is not, however, guaranteed simply by a good match. Which flags the second point here. And an anecdote will perhaps illustrate this second point best. A good friend of mine had a son who had just left acting college and was intent on carving out a career on the stage. I went to see a play he was in at a small London 'fringe' theatre; a production in which the cast were all young people starting out on their careers. His performance – as Macbeth – seemed to me excellent, and I said as much to my friend later. 'What else did you notice?' he asked and, when I could not think what he meant, he commented, 'Everyone in the cast was excellent.' His point was that talent was not going to be the only factor in his son's possible success. He *is* good, but he has to get ahead of a strong field just to work regularly in this field, and certainly to rise to the rank of star. So it is in many fields. Just having the right qualifications and aptitudes is rarely sufficient – others have them too – you have to have them in the right amount and at the right level; and they must show. Then if you work at it (and perhaps have some good luck too, though this is not something to rely on), you may carve out success for yourself. But never make the mistake of thinking this happens in a vacuum – it happens with others around you trying to do similar things. The workplace is inherently competitive. Knowing how well you match up is, nevertheless, a good starting point – one worth some thought.

Sum up your analysis and form clear objectives

As management guru Peter Drucker said in a much-copied phrase about businesses, 'If you do not know where you are going, any road will do.' It is true; you need a plan and having one does make a difference. As with any business – so it is with any career. It's surely no more than common sense, and yet conversely it is so very easy to wake up one day and find that what we have been wont to regard as planning is actually only bowing to the inevitable and, if it looks good, taking the credit for it. Having said that objectives are important, another point should be made: they must be flexible. Life in all its aspects, certainly within organizations, is dynamic. Objectives cannot be allowed to act as a straightjacket, yet we need their guidance, so their potential for acting to fix things should not be regarded as a reason not to have them.

In business, people talk of 'rolling' plans. By this is meant a plan that is reasonably clear and comprehensive for the shorter term, then sets out broad guidelines and further ahead has only main elements clearly stated. As time goes by, the plan can be updated and advanced into the future. With your career in mind, you will find a similar approach works well. In the short term, when you can anticipate more of what may happen, the detail of how you intend to proceed is clearer; further ahead you have notes on the outline strategy and key issues. For instance, remembering to decide: *My objective is to become a marketing director*, is not much help without some clear actions and steps along the way.

Making objectives useful

Objectives should be SMART. This well-known mnemonic stands for specific, measurable, achievable, realistic and timed, thus:

Specific – expressed clearly and precisely.
Measurable – it must be possible to tell if you have achieved something (the difference between saying you want to be 'very successful' or to be 'marketing director').
Achievable – it must not be so difficult as to be pie in the sky; otherwise the plan that goes with it similarly becomes invalid and of no practical help in taking things forward.
Realistic – it must fit with your self-analysis and be what you want; it might be a valid objective to aim for something possible but not ideal (promotion might be possible within a department, but your real intention is to get out beyond that) but this will not be helpful. Action is needed with more ambitious objectives in mind.
Timed – this is important; objectives are not to be achieved 'eventually' but by a particular moment: when do you aim to be marketing director; this year, next year or when?

There is no need for you to complete elaborate documentation here. Any objectives and any plans are purely for your own guidance, but a few notes on paper may be useful and there are times (such as appraisal or when training is contemplated) when it may be useful to think of current events alongside the notes you have made. If you not only know which road you should be on, but have taken steps to make sure you go purposively along it, that is a good start. It certainly helps answer the first two important questions the answers to which help direct your career: *Do you know what you want?* And, *Are you aiming high?*

If you have never thought things through before in this kind of way, then I commend doing so to you. It may take a moment initially, but once done needs little time to keep updated. If you always base all your career management and development activity on such sound analysis, clear thinking and specific objectives then it is more likely that both your long-term action and the way you spot and take advantage of opportunities along the way will take you where you want to go.

Research to assist your progress

There is an important point to accept here, and it is one reinforced by the old saying that 'information is power'. Your career plan can only succeed if it is based on fact. So, you may need to know such things as:

■ what prevailing salary levels are in a particular function or industry;

■ how many companies operate in a certain field or are located in a particular town; or

■ what qualifications are normally essential entry requirements in your kind of job in, say, Australia.

Whatever it is you should check, check carefully and, if necessary, check again. Sources have never been more prolific. If it needs a telephone call, a visit to a good business library or an hour on the internet, so be it. It is your life and career and it is surely too important to base on hunch, hearsay or out-of-date information.

> **!** **ACTION:** Listing the many possible sources that might be relevant to research to assist a career plan is beyond the space and brief here, but some, when you have discovered them, should be noted carefully; you may well need them again.

An action plan

This may well be a plan that you show to no one else. It does not need to be written up like a report, but you should have a record of certain things in writing. Keep this safely, perhaps with other related documents and information (for example, your notes and plans to make your next appraisal meeting go well or your draft CV – the last regularly updated and ready in case you see an opportunity and want to respond quickly).

Do not bury it, even in busy times this plan may be committing you to some action and a date on which it should be done; link with your diary to ensure you remember.

Your plan can only list specifics:

- goals you set yourself (eg to be on the Board by the end of the year);

- stepping stones along the way (eg to join a management committee as the first step to joining the Board);

- means to an end (eg learning to speak French so that you might be considered for posting to the Paris office).

Though it may also be worth listing thoughts *requiring* more work to realize them – *I must find a way to get an opportunity to travel* – and then amending these into more specific objectives.

Future finances

It was announced in the press the other day that less than half the population in the UK is putting any money aside for their retirement. This trend is evident in other countries too. Career and life after that link seamlessly, indeed some people have no cut-off date when they move from work to retirement overnight (for instance, being self-employed and working on various projects I can phase down my work progressively). It may seem a long time until retirement; a time impossible to imagine especially if you are young.

But time passes all too soon. A long-term aspect to the sort of planning described in this chapter can sit comfortably alongside the career issues. You may want to think about savings and pensions (and, in volatile times, alternatives like property investment). You may want to get yourself a good financial advisor as well as stay close to arrangements an employer may provide. Certainly events of the last decade indicate caution, taking nothing for granted and keeping an eye on what is best for you.

One day, perhaps far ahead, you may well bless the fact that you thought carefully about such things and took sensible action accordingly. When you get there, you will find that later stages of life are just as important as earlier ones.

> **!** **ACTION:** This chapter effectively provides a template for a self-analysis exercise. Such things can seem daunting or a chore, but are eminently worthwhile. Once done, and this takes a moment, they are not difficult or time-consuming to update and are with you for life.

With your intentions clear you can turn your attention to how to act to enhance your career situation. A regular foundation for such consideration is the job appraisal meetings that provide stepping stones along the way. In the next chapter we see how they can help and how you can link from them to other things such as development.

4

Job Performance Appraisal

If you want to do something you find a way. If you don't
want to do anything you find an excuse.
— Arab proverb

It is likely that your work is demanding. You no doubt feel you do your best. Maybe your job is satisfying, not least because doing it gives you a sense of achievement. You feel you make things happen, that you make a difference. So, why do you hate the thought of a job appraisal meeting? Once a year, sometimes more, someone sits you down in an office and – this is how it may seem – tells you all the things you are doing wrong, inadequately or failing to do at all. If that is the case no wonder you do not look forward to it.

Yet you should look forward to it, it should be useful; indeed it should be a significant element in monitoring and developing your career.

Job appraisals go with the territory so to speak. Work in an organization of any size and you will have one, if for no other reason than employment legislation prompts most organizations to undertake an appraisal process. But it should, and often is, more than that. And it can be much more. Appraisals represent a unique opportunity to check progress, assess results and look to the future – acting to make it more likely that future performance will not only be satisfactory, but that it will achieve something more. Or they should do. This chapter spells out the background to them; its aim is simple: to help you get more out of your next appraisal. This means not just helping to make the experience easier or more comfortable. Rather, it is to see that more positive action results from it to help make next year's work more satisfying, the desired results more likely to be achieved and, in the long term, that your career progresses satisfactorily.

The nature of the appraisal process

Sometimes job appraisals are not very constructive. Nor are they motivational. If they are not understood, if managers dislike conducting them, or find the process difficult, then they are unlikely to achieve very much. If this is the case then they represent a lost opportunity, because appraisal should be useful to the organization, the appraiser and the appraisee. In this chapter and the next the intention is not to look at how to appraise people, though managers who have this task to do may well find the content useful, but rather to review the experience from the point of view of those being appraised – the appraisees. Going into your next appraisal with the right knowledge and intentions can help make it constructive, helpful and something that helps both your job and your career.

Of course, you are dependent to some extent on the systems used by your employer, and how management implements them. But you can influence the process yourself – maybe to a significant extent. How an appraisal is made constructive matters less than that it is. No one should go blindly into their appraisal meeting hoping for the best and aiming only to 'play it by ear'. It is too important for that. Potentially you have a great deal to gain and it is certainly worth some thought before it begins.

The reasons for job appraisals

The fact that usually you have no choice about whether you attend an appraisal meeting makes considering the reasons the company and the appraiser have for insisting on it a sensible starting point. After all, you do not make all the rules. There is probably a system and forms and procedures that exist and which will be part of what occurs. This does not mean that it is impossible to influence matters, but if you are to do so you need to understand the reasons why things happen the way they do.

Job appraisals may come in many guises. In many organizations this term is sufficient to identify the kind of meeting and process involved. In others there may be other names. These usually involve words like planning, assessment, individual and performance – *Personal performance assessment*, perhaps. Whatever it is called the reasons for its existence are likely to be similar.

Reasons, which should benefit both the individual and the organization, include:

- reviewing the individual's past performance;

- planning their future work and role;

- setting specific individual future goals;

- agreeing and creating individual ownership of such goals;

- identifying development needs and setting up development activity;

- on-the-spot coaching;

- obtaining feedback;

- reinforcing or extending the reporting relationship;

- acting as a catalyst to delegation;

- focusing on longer term career progression;

- Acting to motivate the individual being appraised.

The review may focus on some or all of these; they are not mutually exclusive, but the relative emphasis may well vary. Overall, the intention, through all of the above, is to improve existing performance (taking the view that even good performance can often be improved) and make the likelihood of achieving future plans that much greater.

Clarifying your position

It may be that the first time you hear mention of an organization's appraisal is at a recruitment interview before you take up a job. Certainly on that occasion, or soon after taking up employment, is a good time to ask some questions. Ideally the appraisal will be seen as beneficial for both parties so questions should be well received. It is certainly a reasonable area for a prospective or new employee to investigate.

Consider asking questions such as:

- Will I have a job description?

- How often will I receive an appraisal?

- What form will my appraisal take?

- What topics will be reviewed at appraisal?

- What specific targets form part of the review?

- Is there a standard rating procedure? (maybe you can see, or ask to see, any documentation)

- How does this system relate to salary review?

- What is the link between appraisal and development and training?

- Overall, how will this meeting advance my career?

The answers you receive may be illuminating. If there is clearly no view on this area being important it might even change your view about a prospective employer or manager. It may seem an easy option to escape a real form of assessment, but do you really want to work in an environment where how you are doing is of so little consequence? On the other hand if it transpires that a major part of a future review will centre on the achievement or not of a single specific target, then this too is worth knowing.

You will be able to approach your first appraisal meeting much more easily if you have firm knowledge of its purpose and how it is regarded in the company.

Salary and rewards considerations

It is not strictly the role of appraisals to act in any way to fix salary, or other reward levels, for the future. Having said that, many companies do link appraisals and salary review closely, and – at worst – appraisal is no more than a quick chat followed by the disclosure of what next year's salary is going to be (and sometimes a spirited defence by management as to why it cannot be more). On occasion, and at some levels, much of the meeting can follow a salary announcement and be concerned only with negotiating the levels of salary and rewards; and, yes, let us note firmly here that negotiation is a career skill and one that may assist you in career as well as job terms.

More sensibly many organizations separate the two processes. Appraisal is an objective assessment of work to date and what makes it valuable are the reasons stated earlier. Salary and an assessment of how it should change is another matter, best dealt with at another time. Certainly if it is known that appraisal meetings end with the announcement of a revised salary, then it may distract both the appraiser and the appraisee from concentrating on the issues at hand in the early part of the discussion, and prevent honest and open discussion of any difficulties.

If you want to judge the way your own organization works with regard to appraisals this is one of the factors to check; you may find the actual approach used most constructive when the two factors are separated.

Employment legislation

It is beyond my brief to include a digression and review of all the ins and outs of employment law. Suffice it to say that it is complex, constantly changing and that organizations are very aware that transgressing it can be a time-consuming and costly business. The newspapers regularly bear testimony to the extremes involved, as they bring reports of cases addressing such matters as wrongful dismissal or discrimination, both in the courts and the industrial tribunals that are also involved.

The link here with appraisal is primarily to performance. Ultimately a person's failure to perform can result in dismissal. But what is satisfactory performance and how does an employee know whether they are achieving it or not? The answer needs to involve the formality of job descriptions and appraisal. Simplistically the law makes it difficult to dismiss someone for poor performance if they are able to demonstrate that they have been given no clear definition of their job, or regular ability to know how they are performing. Not unreasonable perhaps. But this link conditions some of the elements of both systems and job descriptions, and appraisals can be deployed only as an insurance against future trouble of this sort.

There is no need to overreact to this picture. Most employers do have constructive reasons apart from this for running an appraisal system, they want to get the most from it and they want it to assist in producing good performance and results in the future. It does no harm, however, to bear this background in mind as part of the picture.

Special factors

A last element to bear in mind as you contemplate the rationale for whatever system your organization uses is how it may relate to particular circumstances. For example, cultural factors vary. Some American-owned organizations have much more formal systems than is usual in the United Kingdom. In other countries the prevailing styles may differ; for instance, such systems in France are very much more concerned with behavioural factors than elsewhere. Some are truly bizarre: I once had contact with an American company who operated a policy they called 'planned insecurity' in their sales department. The person at the bottom of the league each quarter was fired.

Similarly, systems may reflect topical factors. For example, a company may have been taken over and be changing to the system of the new parent; measurement is increased as a prelude to some particular event (this might be positive or negative: the laying off of staff or the expansion of the business).

Again, if you are aware of such factors then you enhance your ability to interact with the system in the right kind of way.

> **!** **ACTION:** Overall, the need is to understand what is being done, why it is being done the way it is, and what attitudes to it, among both appraisers and appraisees, exist. If a little research is necessary to achieve this, then it likely amounts to no more than a few questions and the time taken is minimal.

The personal opportunity

First, you need to be clear in your own mind about how appraisal is regarded by the organization for which you work and by the individual manager who will conduct your appraisal meeting (and note this may mean managers, sometimes more than one is involved). Then you need to think about how it can help *you*. Clearly you need it to be constructive. A 'messy' meeting helps no one, and clarity of purpose is one contributory factor in making it go well.

Specifically, you need to set yourself objectives under a number of headings:

- planning how to make positive points about performance during the period under review;

- being ready to respond to points raised, including negative ones, appropriately;

- projecting the right image;

- reviewing specific work plans for the next period ahead;

- reviewing factors on which success in the future depends;

- identifying the need or desirability for training and development;

- looking ahead to longer term career development;

- linking discussion to salary and benefits review.

You need to think about all of these positively. Appraisals are rightly described as an opportunity. What needs to be done is not simply to think broadly about the sort of year it has been overall, but to have clear intentions regarding *what* needs to be (or will inevitably be) discussed and about *what you can get from the discussion.*

The first two points above – essentially planning how you will handle the points discussed, either about the past or future – will be left on one side for the moment. The other points are reviewed here, in turn.

Projecting the right image

The attitude you take to this spans the whole process. It may help to think about it in two ways, the image you project in terms of your:

■ **Attitude to the appraisal:** Here you need to make sure that it is clear that you accept and understand the need for appraisal, that you are approaching it constructively and that you intend to ensure that it helps you produce a good performance in the next period. You are unlikely to impress an appraiser if you seem resentful of the process, take a negative view or are inappropriately defensive. It is easy to overreact to criticism – and realistically there may well be some – and you need to state your side of things, but you may also need to accept and agree that some things were not perfect and move on to other matters.

■ **Attitude to the job:** Remember that how you are perceived has a direct bearing on your job prospects, everything from the likelihood of your taking on a little more responsibility to you being promoted. Remember too that people extrapolate their perceptions. Arrive ill-prepared for your appraisal and you may find that you are not just seen as momentarily disorganized with regard to an important occasion, but that assumptions are made that you are generally poorly organized in the way you do your job. Such a view might directly influence decisions about your future.

So, consider how you want to be seen (this is useful beyond appraisal). You may want to be seen as knowledgeable, expert, capable, innovative or creative, good with people and at communicating, efficient and productive, well organized, reliable, giving appropriate attention to detail, confident, or any or all of these and more. You may want such factors to come over in a very specific way: displaying impressive knowledge of computer systems, perhaps, or being able not just to communicate but produce the best written report style in the office.

> **!** **ACTION:** If you think about it, not only are there a fair number of points in such a list, but they are also all things you can elect to project. For example, you may not be naturally well organized, you work hard at it and manage to achieve what you want, but on occasions such as appraisals you make sure there is no chance you will be mistaken for someone disorganized. The moral here is to make sure you think through, in sufficient detail, how you want to come over and make doing so an active process.

Reviewing specific work plans

Here you need to focus on the job you do and what doing it will entail in future. Maybe you are about to embark on managing a particular project. This might entail liaison with others, tight deadlines or push you into areas beyond your current experience. If so, consider what help, advice or support you might find useful from your manager and use the appraisal to touch on the process. It is unlikely to be the occasion to discuss such matters in detail, you could seek to set up another meeting for that, but having the fact of it on the table, as it were, may influence other elements of your discussion.

Reviewing success criteria

This links closely with the above heading and you need to think about what your job will entail over the coming months, and what factors are involved that affect your potential success. Maybe economic conditions are changing and you feel targets should too. Or staffing changes are planned that will tie up time on handover activity. Or systems changes will mean time needs to be spent on training or running things in.

The examples above are negative. That is, they might hinder your ability to do the job. Positive factors may need discussion also. For example, systems changes might free up time and provide the opportunity for you to take additional initiatives elsewhere.

In either case, it may be useful at a later date to be able to link a request for support to even an overall intention agreed at appraisal.

Training and development

This should be a mandatory topic for any appraisal. In most organizations it pays to be seen as keen on training (and from a career point of view actually keen on it too, of course). It is potentially useful. Indeed, given the dynamic world in which we all live, it is sensible to assume that whatever skills you have will not see you through an entire career, but that they will need updating and extending on a regular basis.

Training can be viewed in two ways:

■ **Immediate needs:** those things that link very specifically the current job and the work over the coming months. If you know you are going to have to undertake many more formal presentations in future, for instance, and do not feel sufficient confidence in your ability to do them well, then appraisal is a good time to aim to get agreement to attend a course.

■ **Longer term needs:** here you may see a longer term need and consider it worth making a start on whatever it is sooner rather than later; and certainly instead of having to do something in a rush later. Or you may simply want to extend your competencies, abilities and perspective with a general eye on the future. Organizations will often accommodate both, though perhaps it is easier to gain agreement to the former, so again you can form specific intentions as to what you want to achieve.

Remember, training and development encompass a wide range of different activities, literally from reading a book (even a short one like this!) to attending a course of sufficient duration to cause problems to continuity and your ability to keep things moving while you are away. Be realistic. You are not going to get permission to spend three months in an American Business School *every* year, but you should aim at agreeing some mix of development activity on a regular basis. Appraisal is also a good moment for some feedback, and perhaps some appreciation, about past training and its usefulness.

Aim high. It is better to suggest more training than is approved, than to have no ideas about any, and it is easier to trade down than up.

Linking to career development

It is always sensible to have an active plan for the development of your career. This involves assessing your strengths and weaknesses, looking at what direction you would like to take and what might be necessary to allow you to take it. From your point of view progress may ultimately take you away from your existing employer. If this is a firm intention, it may not be a suitable topic for discussion at an appraisal. However, the longer term possibilities do need some discussion, and consideration is necessary here if you are to agree matters that may form important stepping stones along the way.

Such matters may initially be minor, say a small involvement with another department or activity. Or they may involve, or set up, much more of a jump ahead. You might know what you want to do in this regard, and want to discuss it or push for it. Alternatively you might be at the stage where an appraisal meeting is an opportunity to get some advice or start a longer term dialogue. In such discussions, remember to emphasize the gains to the organization of changes you suggest, rather than simply saying that it is good for you.

Again, having specific objectives in mind is important. Just planning to say 'What about the long term?' may take you into a substantial and useful digression, but it might only prompt a brief comment and a return to the next topic. Such a question does not constitute a true objective. Remember that any objective needs to be specific, preferably measurable and linked to clear timing. So you may need to lead in with something that begins more like this: 'In two years time I would hope to be doing..., to have a salary of..., and be in line for (the next step up). How can we...?' Aiming high is good, but at the same time you must select steps that are likely to be achievable (not: 'How do I become MD within the year?'). And you need to make your aims realistic (for example: not aiming in a direction that clearly needs special skills you do not have, at least without including something about their acquisition).

This is an important area, and one that it is easy to give too little attention to in the face of more immediate pressures. Yet the worst position to get yourself into is one where you look back and say to yourself 'If only...'. There is a line in one of John Lennon's songs that says 'Life is what happens while you are making other plans.' Not a pleasant thought. The moral is always to balance your short- and long-term thinking and action about the future.

Rewards

This goes hand in hand with appraisal, although – as has been said – the actual decisions may be separated. However it is handled in your organization never go into an appraisal meeting without some sensible thoughts and intentions about salary and benefits. Again, aiming high is fine, but specific objectives are essential. It does not help you to decide how to raise or deal with matters if you simply say to yourself 'I want as big an increase as possible' (even if this means it will prove true!). You need to think about things in context (inflation, the levels paid to your peers and in other companies etc). And remember that reward packages are complex these days. More money is something most people want, but changes to a range of things from car schemes to pensions also have monetary consequences, and it pays to keep the broad picture in mind.

There is obviously a range of things that need consideration here. Some relate one to another, like new responsibilities and training that makes you able to take them on. Some have topical importance; others have longer term implications. There is too much at stake to rely on only a brief moment's thinking ahead of the meeting seeing you through, and the last thing you want is to come out of so important a meeting and remember something you wanted to raise and simply forgot.

If you are clear in your mind, and sensibly have made some notes, too, about what you want to achieve in all these areas, then you can proceed to more formal preparation with that in mind. It may seem to indicate a greater task than it does. In reality, this thinking is something undertaken on a rolling basis. For the most part you are updating a pre-existing picture rather than starting with a blank sheet of paper, and this helps keep the process manageable. Whatever thinking through is entailed to clarify the range of objectives you then use, however, it is likely to prove worthwhile. Such thinking is the first step in ensuring you get the most from your appraisal.

The necessary information

Appraisals are most likely to be constructive when they concentrate not just on broad issues, but also on specifics: what actually was done, how it was done and what results were achieved. But a great deal can happen during the course of a year. Try an experiment. Try to recall what you were doing in a particular week – pick one at random, maybe nine months ago. Even if you consult your diary, your recollections may be less than perfect.

One of the things that may occur during an appraisal meeting is precisely this. You will be asked to recall something from the past and comment on it – how a project went, say. And you may not always get notice of what aspects of the last year's events this will relate to. However a topic comes up for discussion, introduced unexpectedly or with some notice or suggested by you as a significant event worthy of consideration as an example of how things have gone over the past year, you need to have some details of it.

Perfect recollection is clearly not possible. No one recalls every detail of everything with which they have been involved. But some firm basis of recall is clearly useful. This may apply to details such as your diary. A day that notes: *10am meeting with PF re: project progress*, may have been highly informative the day before, but mean nothing six months on. Some vigilance in such matters may well be useful, but something more formal is also sensible, because the foundation of a successful appraisal meeting is good information.

Assembling supporting information

Appraisal collection file

Appraisal schemes are usually accompanied by documentation (more of this later), so having a file relating to your past appraisals is logical enough. Simply dividing it into past and future sections can help you ensure the next one goes well.

The starting point is the documentation from your last appraisal. From then on you should make a point of collecting into that file documents (or copies of documents – their first purpose may suggest another file as their main resting-place) that have a bearing on your next meeting. These will include:

- a note of any courses you go on (as a minimum, file a copy of the course outline and a copy of any evaluation form you may have been asked to complete, perhaps together with a note of where any résumé notes are to be found);

- a note of any 'significant events'; these might include something about what was your first presentation, say, or the fact that you spoke at a trade association meeting or joined a significant committee;

- notifications of targets set, progress against them and ultimate results achieved;

- comments made by other people: maybe the MD wrote you a letter of congratulations about something, or a satisfied customer put pen to paper about service you delivered.

Other useful documents might be any memos, minutes of meetings or other documents that are a record of your activity and outputs.

The idea is not to hoard everything or spend a long time amassing this; a note rather than a whole document may well be sufficient. You can sensibly match the information you gather to the topics that you know will feature in your forthcoming review. For example, if you are judged in part on your communications skills, keep some evidence of them.

Remember that this is not solely a 'boasting file' containing references to your successes. If things do go wrong, or less well than you had hoped, they may well be subject to review also – this extends the information you can usefully collect.

Background information

In addition to the kinds of things mentioned, there are various other items that may be added as backup. Key amongst these is your *job description*. This is not a formality, although employment legislation and sometimes heavy-handed Personnel practice can sometimes make it so; it is a working tool. Everyone needs a clear brief as to what their job entails (and maybe what lies outside its jurisdiction). In many companies, certainly at departmental level, job descriptions – if necessary minus any confidential information (about salary grades, say) – are circulated. This means that members of a team see exactly how responsibilities fit together, something that should include the manager of the section. This is something that you might bring up at an appraisal meeting as a means of clarifying matters and ensuring effective teamwork.

Sometimes appraisals use the structure and content of a job description as an element of their agenda, if so it is useful to have this in mind, but if not, then you may want to refer to areas included in the description but not mentioned.

Think about any other documentation that your own role might make useful, for example:

- financial results (especially when they form, even in part, a basis for your evaluation);

- standing or exceptional instructions;

- records indicating factors that have changed during the year;

■   notes following any less formal evaluation or coaching that may have taken place during the year.

If this sort of appraisal collection file is kept up to date and in order, then it can act as a useful reference when you come to prepare for your next appraisal meeting. There is one key reason for all this – the avoidance of argument. It is all too easy for appraisals to deteriorate into a 'table tennis match' of 'it was/it wasn't' arguments if any key facts are subject to misinterpretation or dispute. It benefits both parties, and makes the meeting much more likely to be constructive, if facts are clear to all. You cannot necessarily rely on your appraiser to produce the memo that you know shows results improved by 12.7 per cent, you are just as likely to have them saying 'Well, figures were only up 10 per cent or so'; and the difference may be important.

The intention here is to ensure a constructive base for the meeting. It is not intended to suggest that there is a need for elaborate defences against appraisers eager to 'do you down'. But some of the points made here apply equally to appraisers. If it is difficult for you to remember the detail of what you have been up to all year, how much more difficult is it for a manager who has 8 or 10 people reporting to them to do so?

> **!**   **ACTION:** The overall moral here is that you cannot hope for a satisfactory experience of appraisal just by 'winging it'; information must be to hand and if this demands organization and research, so be it.

The overriding intention commended in this chapter is to play your part in ensuring that there is a sound basis of pertinent, accurate information for you to draw on as your appraisal approaches.

5

Surviving and Benefiting from Appraisal

No one can make you feel inferior without your consent.
— Eleanor Roosevelt

With the background described in the last chapter out of the way, let's consider the actual process in three stages:

1. preparing for the meeting;

2. participating in the meeting; and

3. what action follows from it.

Preparation logically comes first.

1. Preparing for appraisal

Your appraisal is too important to simply try to 'wing' it on the day. Preparation is surely necessary if you are to get the most from the process. Yet preparation is essentially no more than a formalized version of the age-old advice to engage the brain before the mouth. It need not be daunting, and it need not take too long.

Take the initiative

Amongst the guidelines given to any manager about conducting appraisals will be the need to give appraisees adequate advance notice. Surprise is not intended to be part of the procedure. Rather it is intended that appraisal meetings review the considered thoughts of both parties. You should get adequate warning and an agenda, setting out content and sequence (and giving an idea of how long the meeting is expected to last) and – depending on the system being used – you may be asked to complete a form and return it ahead of the meeting. If the latter is the case then you have a formal opportunity to set down something about your performance.

All this may well happen. If so, then that's all well and good. The occasion is sufficiently important to you, however, for you to take an initiative if this is not the case. You can:

- ask in advance when an appraisal is to be scheduled (and maybe ask for some of the attendant information such as the duration of the meeting as you do so);

- respond to any brief notification by asking for additional detail, specifying points such as:

  - duration;

  - location;

  - agenda etc.

You could also ask to have included any items that you feel will be useful. If such a request is made positively – *perhaps I may suggest that it might be useful to…* – there is no reason why it should not be taken that way. If you want due consideration of points you raise it may be better to put them in writing rather than simply stick your head round someone's door and say, 'Do you have a minute?'

Conversely, you can be sure that if you simply arrive at the meeting and then start asking for changes and additions to the agenda it will be likely to cause problems.

Note particularly any areas where clarification is necessary ahead of the meeting (or perhaps as is starts), decide how and when you will check them out and take the necessary action. One example, which may be important, is confidentiality. Before you speak out you need to know how this is regarded. Care spent on this sort of reconnaissance is always worthwhile.

Dealing with systems

Appraisals need a systematic approach. Without any system the review would become very subjective, and then it would be difficult to ensure that it was either thorough or fair. Because of this most organizations have thought through both the topics and headings under which they will evaluate performance, and the rating scales used to actually record a judgement on standards of performance. This is reflected in the forms and formats that you will find being used during the process.

Usually such documentation is divided into two distinct sections: one concerned with the past and a review of past performance, and the other concerned with a preview of the future. The first of these, as has been mentioned, may be used to collect your own initial evaluation ahead of the meeting.

Systems vary, not least in the amount of detail they are designed to collect, and many are tailored to reflect the nature of particular jobs and the tasks they entail. The checklist that follows summarizes typical areas scheduled for review:

CHECKLIST: Appraisal form

Reviewing past performance

Agenda: the first questions may be linked to finalizing the meeting:

- What do you want to come from this meeting?

- Are there special areas you would like to spend time on? – and why?

Job: here questions focus on the task in hand, both *qualitatively* with questions about what you like, have enjoyed or found satisfying or challenging (or a problem); and *quantitatively* with questions about successes, and results and targets met or missed.

Relationships: investigating your work in terms of how it interacts with other people (whether peers, subordinates or those elsewhere in the organization – or outside it – with whom you must work or liaise).

Development: this heading allows a focus on skills: what is needed for the job now, how you rate yourself at them, and whether there are skills which need adding or extending (or which are not currently being utilized).

Personal: an opportunity to think about things more in terms of feelings: have things been easy or difficult? Would you do things differently if it were possible? Are you being stretched, are you learning or getting into a rut?

Special projects: some such heading allows specific, or more topical, areas of your work to be discussed.

Planning for future success

This section should rate at least half the discussion and time (possibly more). The focus is on the next period ahead and the way in which the chances of achieving success during it can be strengthened. Often the same main headings repeat, and questions need to allow:

- changes and differences that are known or can be anticipated (year on year);

- ideas for improvement that might become part of next year's way of working;

- priorities for the period;

- your role and how it might change.

Always respect the system. Even if you do not like it you may be unable to change it, and any action you do take to see it amended in some way might be better kept separate from the cycle of your own appraisal. It is one thing to suggest going beyond the system, indeed the system may allow for this by specifically asking you for additional suggestions for discussion, but it is quite another to ignore elements of it without good reason.

Some companies accompany their appraisal materials with a 'guidance for appraisees' document. If you are given something like this always take time to read it carefully. Also, whether you have such notes or not, if you do not understand some aspect of the system *always ask*; and do so in good time. It helps no one to go into your review unclear in some way as to what is expected of you.

Rating scales

An inherent part of the appraisal format is likely to be rating scales. These take many forms and so too do the way organizations interpret them. Some may link them precisely to specific outcomes (including salary judgements); others use them less formally, with one end of the scale implying no action and the other some degree of corrective action.

Scales are *not* only there to flag the poorer performance or identify weaknesses (though they do that); it may be as useful – or more so – to explore what creates good performance and see if there are lessons to be learnt from it or passed round the organization.

The scales should certainly be studied, therefore. The following shows some of the formats you will perhaps encounter:

- **Simple numeric scale:** 1–6, 1–7 or whatever, with one end being positive and the other negative (these could alternatively use labels such as A, B, C etc).

- **Descriptive scale:** this may or may not be linked to numbers and the words may or may not be chosen with precision: eg Excellent, Very good, Good, Fair, Adequate, Unsatisfactory.

- **Graphic scale:** this is effectively just a line with identified positive and negative ends: eg HIGH -------------------------------- LOW and perhaps with mid or quarter points shown.

- **Comparative scale:** this might be a list of perhaps 4 to 10 statements: phrases such as 'Better than most in the group'.

- **Behavioural scale:** this rates a list of options that specifically relates to things done, specifying them, for example, as Always, Almost always, Usually, Infrequently or Never done.

Essentially all serve the same purpose, and also act to ensure consistency and fairness – that is, all people are assessed in the same kind of way and each person is rated in a way that allows comparisons year on year. *Note:* the most important aspect of ratings is a line beyond which action is necessary – and thus prompted – when performance fails to reach a required level.

!   **ACTION:** It may be worth thinking about specific topics you believe will be discussed in terms of whatever ratings are used. Some answers or comments may usefully start with a phrase like, 'I think I rate XX in terms of this project, because...'

Some preparation here can create fluency.

So, study the system, complete and return any forms – on time – and set aside some private time too to consider the detail of what your appraisal might, will, or should involve and help you make it work for *you*.

Think ahead

Systems apart, appraisals should be conversations. They may, however, cover a wealth of detail and last from an hour or so to two or three hours (or longer). It is a mistake to think you will remember everything that you want to ask or mention as the meeting goes along, and annoying to realize later that you have forgotten to raise a key issue as you intended.

All that is necessary is some thought and a few notes.

Keep the format of the appraisal in mind. After the first one with a particular employer you have a reasonable idea of how it will be done, and the first-time questions can ensure it is not totally unknown territory. For example, if you know you are likely to be asked some introductory and broad-based question to start with – 'All in all, how would you describe the year?' – then how you encapsulate matters may stand some thought. A good turn of phrase may help get the meeting off to a good start and also help you establish the focus you want. *Note:* This is also an opportunity to introduce specific topics. You might say such things as, 'I believe it's been a good year, certainly projects such as X and Y produced good results and extended my abilities too.'

Beyond that you need to consider systematically (and with the system in mind) a number of factors to help you through the meeting:

■   **The topics you want to discuss:** these may be well described by the agenda and appraisal forms, but you may wish to add to or amend the list.

■   **Examples within each topic:** for example, if your project management skills are to be discussed, then you may want to select one or more examples of what you have done during the year, and note specifically *how* you made them go well (choose one that did!), and what the outcomes were at the end. If you know examples will be raised of things not going so well, do not just amass excuses, think what came out of it that was positive – what did you learn? How much better would something similar go next time?

■ **Detailed points:** think also how you want to exemplify or describe the detail arising from the discussion, and *how* exactly you want to make the point. The same action could be described as taking place because of your excellent planning, or as a result of your inherent flexibility and ability to respond promptly and intelligently to unforeseen occurrences.

■ **Areas for questioning:** and perhaps the actual questions you want to ask. Well-phrased questions speak of planning and a considered approach and this may be what you want. Not least, the job here is to discover what you want quickly and easily in a way that does not disrupt the agenda or take up too much time.

There is no need for secrecy about all this incidentally: if you find it useful to sit down in the meeting with some notes – and even a file of exhibits – in front of you, then you should do so. You do not want to either forget something or handle it inappropriately; and the appraiser will approve of your preparation.

Although you can never anticipate everything and planning must never be a straightjacket, a sound plan will make it more likely that you will handle the meeting well and that you will cope with any unforeseen circumstances along the way as well.

One last point: if you have thought through things in this kind of way you will feel more confident about the meeting. They can seem stressful occasions; after all, there may be a good deal hanging on them. But stress is a reaction. A difficult meeting you have not planned is certainly likely to worry you. A well-planned meeting, one that you have confidence in your ability to handle, is more likely to go well.

2. Participating in the appraisal meeting

Now, the moment arrives. You are in the hot seat, and you have to do your best to make the meeting itself go well. As the last section explained, preparation is vital. A deep breath as you walk through the door is unlikely to be sufficient, but there are certainly things that, when you get to this stage, you can do to assist in making the process go well. None of the detail that follows is itself complex. But appraisals, like many meetings for that matter, do require the orchestration of a number of different elements. The complexity – and the need for care – is more in this overall orchestration than in any one individual area. The better you understand the nature of the meeting, and all that needs to or might go on in it, the easier this orchestration will be.

First impressions last

Any injunction about first impressions is likely to seem to be something of a cliché. That may be. But the point remains; if everything gets off to a good start, then this gives you greater confidence and acts to continue to keep the meeting on track.

Several things are worth bearing in mind at this stage. They include:

■   **Appearance:** you need to look the part. I would not presume to tell you how to dress. Suffice to say that this is not a good day to find your suit looks as if it was slept in (or was!) or that you are at the end of six weeks of saying, 'I really must get my hair cut.'

■   **Manner:** this too is a personal matter, though worth a moment's thought. You may well have your appraisal conducted by someone you know well; the manager you work with day to day. But it could be someone else, perhaps more senior, perhaps less well known to you; and it could, in some organizations, involve two people or even a panel. Do not overreact and take the meeting as having to be very formal, but adjust your level of familiarity or flippancy as seems appropriate.

■   **Procedure:** if necessary, take the initiative and double-check anything unknown, for instance about the agenda, format or duration for the meeting. This should have been spelt out in advance; if not, such things are best clarified at the start.

Then relax. This is a meeting that is designed to help you and to benefit the organization. It should be interesting, it should be constructive and it may even be stimulating. Approach it as such, rather than with doom and gloom or too much apprehension, and it is likely to go better. Let any reservations you have about it show and that alone could change the attitude an appraiser takes to you.

Once the meeting is under way there are several techniques that you will need to deploy – all with your objectives in mind, and in a way that reacts intelligently to what occurs (which will never be exactly as you predicted). Prime are your abilities to listen, to ask questions, to comment, deal with any criticism, and pick up and link to any opportunities presented.

These techniques are now considered in turn.

Listening

Of course you listen. Really? Never had a breakdown in communications because you did not really take something in properly? Honestly? If you want to demonstrate to yourself how listening varies in effectiveness, just consider what happens when someone says something that you disagree with. At once your mind begins to spend some of its power, not on listening, but on developing a counter argument. The effect of this can be pronounced.

Not only do you want to take in clearly everything that is said to you in an appraisal, you want to *appear* to be a good listener, one who takes the proceedings seriously. The checklist that follows sets out some principles that are useful and which certainly show listening to be an active process.

CHECKLIST: Effective listening

■ **Want to listen:** recognizing how it can help you is the first step to doing it well.

■ **Look like a good listener:** let the appraiser see they have your attention by appropriate eye contact and acknowledgement of what is said to you.

■ **Listen and stop talking:** you cannot do both at once, the meeting will become awkward and you need to resist the temptation to interrupt, waiting until the point is fully made (or what you do will seem like evasion).

■ **Use empathy:** put yourself in the other person's shoes, try to see things from their point of view and make it clear you are doing so.

■ **Check:** clarify as you go along if anything is not clear, leaving it can simply build up bigger problems later.

■ **Remain calm:** concentrate on the facts and try not to let over-reaction, or becoming emotional, hinder your ability to take in the full message.

■ **Concentrate:** and allow nothing to distract you.

■ **Focus on key points:** get to the nub of what is being said, which may be buried in other, less important, information and comment.

■ **Avoid personalities:** concentrate on what is said – the argument – rather than who is saying it.

■ **Take one thing at a time:** jumping ahead, especially if you do so on the basis of assumption, can cause problems.

■ **Avoid negative reactions:** certainly initially; hear the comment out and do not look horrified (even if you are!) ahead of working out how you intend to proceed.

> **Make notes:** do not trust your memory, jot down key points as the meeting proceeds (and, if you feel it is polite or necessary, ask permission to do so).
>
> *Note:* Listening is not just important to appraisal; it is a career skill, one that affects how you are perceived and is worth taking care with in many contexts.

Perhaps all this should go without saying, but it is easy to find yourself regarding an appraisal as a rather traumatic occasion, at least to some extent, and forgetting to handle things thoroughly.

Questions

There is no rule about the order here. Sometimes you will be asked questions or be on the receiving end of comments to which you must respond. But you may need to respond to such with a question – indeed there is often no reason why a question cannot be answered by a question – and there will be occasions during the meeting when you should lead in this way. The alternative is to find you are off target and not talking about what is really required.

Questions can easily be ambiguous (this is possible whoever puts them). This is something that leads us back to preparation. Part of the time before the meeting may usefully be spent not only thinking of what you might ask, but how you can put it clearly and succinctly. Some thought here is well worthwhile, as confusion can annoy and waste time.

Three types of question can be used:

■ **Closed questions:** these are questions that can be answered easily with a quick 'Yes' or 'No'. As such they are most useful for checking facts and leading into deeper areas of investigation. But otherwise their use may be limited, especially when a fuller answer is sought.

■   **Open questions:** these cannot be answered with a simple 'Yes' or 'No'. They are designed to get people talking, to elucidate real information and detail – they typically start with the words: what, why, when, where, how and who and with phrases such as 'Tell me about...' (the latter may not technically be a question, but does get people talking).

The difference between these two approaches is marked. Ask 'Will I be able to take on new things next year?' (or specify a particular area of work), and the answer may well be 'Yes'. But if the conversation then moves on, there is little you have really discovered. When will a new involvement start? How will it be initiated? What will it involve? And so on. However, ask, 'Tell me something about any new involvements you see me taking on next year' and the subsequent conversation may explain much more.

■   **Probing questions:** sometimes even an open question does not produce everything you want. Then you need to be prepared to pursue a point, asking a series of questions to focus on a particular area and get to the required level of detail. Phrases like 'Tell me *more* about...', or 'Can you explain that further' may make a good start.

> **!   ACTION:** Questions are of major significance. Have good ones ready, and do not be afraid to refer to them ('There were specific questions I wanted to ask about this, let me just check'); doing so is evidence of being well prepared.

Making comments

Appraisals demand you comment on your work and performance. This is what your preparation should have addressed. Your objectives are perhaps to maximize the impressiveness of what you describe and minimize anything negative. You may receive some criticism – more of this later.

The key issues are again common sense:

■ **Be clear:** follow all the rules of good communication; do not go round the houses, beware of inappropriate jargon and get your point across succinctly. This may seem the simplest part of the proceedings, but it is worth some thought. Remember you probably know a good deal more about the details of your job than the appraiser. Remember too that clarity, especially where complexity is expected, impresses.

■ **Be descriptive:** is it sufficient to say you 'made a plan', or better to say what kind of plan it was – practical, excellent, creative (cunning? – maybe not)? And if it is a creative plan, maybe you should explain – describe – how. Use some well-chosen adjectives to support what you say. There is no reason why you cannot use some visual aids if they would help. Do not struggle to describe complex figures, for example, if one glance at a pie chart would allow the appraiser to see the point in a moment.

■ **Concentrate on implications and results:** do not just comment on *what* happened or was done; rather describe *how* it was done and especially what *came from it*. For instance, perhaps you saw to the production of a new corporate brochure. You can just mention this, or you can mention how it was produced, your copywriting skills, the deadline being hit or bettered, the way checking out several printers saved money, and the positive reaction expressed by customers about it – or even the business that has already resulted from it. All the later points can be chosen to link in with your agenda and objectives and how you want to put things over.

■ **Provide proof:** where necessary do not just say what happened, but demonstrate it, documenting evidence or quoting figures where appropriate. Incidentally, figures that may often be used in evidence must always be quoted appropriately. It may be sufficient to say 'the increase was around 10 per cent', but better to say 'productivity went up 11.8 per cent' (and never say 'about 10.7 per cent', the juxtaposition of the word 'about' and a precise figure just does not work).

Dealing with criticism

Badly conducted appraisals will often focus almost exclusively on the things that have gone less than perfectly. At worst the conversation then deteriorates into an argument and as things are banged to and fro nothing very much is achieved.

But any appraisal is going to spend time on difficulties – it goes with the territory so to speak – and you must be ready to deal with this. Three intentions should be uppermost in your mind in this respect, over and above a general desire to put the best complexion on everything.

■ **Achieving accuracy:** here your intention is to ensure that the right facts are considered. Beware of the appraiser using vague statements like 'You're never on time with anything.' This is unlikely to be true. But what are you late with and what are the implications? It is easier to discuss specifics and questions may well be the route to identify them.

Never argue with anything but the true facts; checking what is really meant is the first step to responding to what is said in the right way.

■ **Giving an impression of objectivity:** if every criticism is seen simply to put you into automatic defensive mode, then discussion will be unlikely to be constructive. Using an acknowledgement to position what follows is always useful. It:

- indicates that you feel there is a point to discuss (if you do not, then we are back to achieving accuracy – see above);

- shows that you are not going to argue unconstructively;

- makes it clear that you intend to respond in a serious and considered fashion;

- gives you a moment to think (which may be very useful!) and sets up the subsequent discussion so that you can handle it better.

Just a few words may be all that is necessary here. Starting with a 'yes' gives it power – *Yes, there was a problem with that* – and sounds right even if your intention is to go on to minimize the problem.

■   **Dealing with the points raised:** now the job is to deal with the matter. Mechanistically the options are few and therefore manageable. If you need to explain why a difficulty occurred, then there are four routes to handling things:

1. *Remove the difficulty:* if possible, you can explain that what seemed like a difficulty or error was not in fact that. A delay, say, might not have been in an original plan, but caused little problem.

2. *Reduce the difficulty:* maybe you have to acknowledge that there was some difficulty, but explain that it was of little significance.

3. *Turn the difficulty into a plus:* sometimes it is possible to argue that what might initially seem like a problem is in fact not. A delay might not have been in an original plan, but included for a positive reason – there might only have been a real problem *without* the delay.

4. *Agree the difficulty:* after all, there is no point in trying to argue that black is white. Most ordinary mortals have some problems during a whole year of activity. Your job is not to persuade the appraiser that there were *no* problems, but to persuade the appraiser that, on balance, your year was a good one.

Remember that the prime purpose of appraisal is to set the scene for successful work in the *coming* year, not argue about what cannot be changed. None of us can turn the clock back, but all of us can learn from experience. So the key thing to include when the discussion touches on difficulties, is the lessons that have been learnt for the future.

The list of implications and actions here is considerable. Failure may have come about because of unforeseen circumstances (and new procedures are necessary in case such circumstances occur again). You may be starting to have to use skills not previously necessary in the job (and training may be needed to quickly add them to your portfolio). You may have made a simple slip (and only need to make a firm mental note not to let it happen again). There may be lessons to learn, but ultimately the emphasis needs to be on what happens next, and this allows a return to the most constructive elements of the dialogue.

> **!** **ACTION:** If there is one area that needs particular preparation it is in your response to criticism. You will surely know what is likely to be raised: be ready for such topics and have a constructive response ready.

Note: if you have made gross errors you may find that your appraisal overlaps into a discipline procedure. Similarly, your appraisal may be the first occasion on which you raise matters such as discrimination that is, in turn, linked to employment legislation. The details of both discipline procedures and of complex employment law are beyond the scope of this short text; if necessity arises do investigate them separately.

A final point here: the constructive approach commended as a response to criticism is something that can be usefully deployed in many ways, formally and informally.

Targets

When considering results it should be recognized that in any particular job some targets may well be sacrosanct. They may also link directly and automatically to the way you are rated, and indeed paid. Fail to hit a sales target, say, or a particular level of productivity and specific sanctions may cut in. Again the conclusion may be only that this goes with the territory. Appraisals take a view of the job as it is and judge performance accordingly.

It may be that circumstances or events lead to conclusions being drawn, or action decided upon, that change some of the seemingly fixed parameters. In this case documentation, for instance a change to the written job description, may be necessary.

Ratings

Where appropriate, ratings used for formal measurement during appraisal may need noting (perhaps completing a form) as the appraisal proceeds; alternatively this may be done at the end of the meeting. Some of these may be linked to targets and, as such, can be pre-judged; ie a failure to hit a target is known in advance of the meeting and thus the outcome is known too. Essentially though, the judgements should be made *during* the meeting and, as it may not be known *why* something occurred, the discussion is needed to allow a fair judgement to be made.

Opportunities

Always be on the lookout for opportunities. Circumstances and attitudes that come to light during the meeting may create a new view of something. A new involvement may come out of a project handled during the year that seemed only a distraction. Yet, well handled, it throws up discussions about capabilities that you have displayed, which would not otherwise have been seen. And this in turn allows discussion to investigate new paths for the future.

Sometimes you can spot and lead into such a discussion. Sometimes the appraiser does so; maybe incorporating information you knew nothing of beforehand. In the latter case you have to be sure you see what is happening and link it to your own aims and objectives.

Action plans

All appraisal meetings benefit from a clear summary. You may be asked to do this or to comment and add to the appraiser's summary. At this stage, ratings apart, one of the most important issues to be clear about is the definition of any action plans that are being put together.

These may be specific and firm – you are to commence sitting on a management committee from their meeting on 15 December, say. Or they may be an initial idea that needs following up. In the latter case all that can be made specific is the arrangements for a further meeting to investigate further or tie things down. On some topics, it may be a better outcome for you to have an additional and separate meeting set, than to insist on lengthy discussion at the time that disrupts the agenda and timing for the whole appraisal.

Do not forget

Whatever happens, and sometimes appraisal meetings do get a little emotional, *always keep your cool*. Never overreact. Certainly you can, on occasion, be assertive – probably your appraiser expects no less. You must have the courage of your convictions about things, but your image will suffer if you get angry or upset where this is inappropriate. If necessary take a deep breath and never be afraid to say 'Perhaps I may think about that for a moment' as you collect your thoughts. What are wanted are your considered views, not rash outbursts.

At the end

So, at the end of the session you can leave the meeting with:

- a constructive discussion behind you;

- ratings agreed and documented;

- a development plan updated;

- some lessons learnt and noted;

- plans laid and dates set for the coming period; and maybe

- additional time scheduled for further discussions of specific issues – indeed, ensuring that this happens is a prime career-building activity.

Whatever else, and however good or bad the appraisal might have been, you can leave with a personal profile that is positive in a number of ways, for example in your:

- attitude to the appraisal;

- conduct and constructive attitude during it;

- willingness to accept constructive criticism and learn from it;

- ability to identify and focus on the key results areas;

- likelihood of being able to deliver a good performance next year.

All over? Forget about it all until the same time next year? No, there is just a little more to be considered if you are going to maximize any advantage that you can obtain from your appraisal.

3. Action after the meeting

Phew! The meeting is over. Maybe it was not as daunting as you thought it would be. Maybe it went well. However it may have turned out, there is a temptation to heave a sigh of relief, put the whole thing on one side and get on with the job. To do so is almost certainly a mistake. There is more to do, and consideration of this is worth a moment's thought.

The appraisal cycle

Before turning to the practical action needed after an appraisal meeting, consider the cycle of events of which appraisal is part. The cycle of action necessary to ensure ongoing good performance flows as follows:

- **Job definition:** the first task is to define the job in terms of its objectives and tasks and any attendant matters: the relationships it involves, the boundaries and overlaps with other jobs etc.

- **Capabilities definition:** this defines the knowledge, skills and attitudes that it is necessary for someone to have to be able to do justice to the job.

- **Assessment of the *actual* level of capabilities:** in other words the level of knowledge, skills and attitudes that an individual has currently.

- **Identify changes:** additional or extended knowledge, skills and attitudes that the job may demand looking ahead to what it will involve in future.

- **Set developmental objectives:** decide what action may be necessary to close any gap between the existing level of capabilities and what is actually needed.

- **Set priorities:** decide what must be done first, second and so on.

- **Implement development activities:** carry out the planned activity.

- **Evaluate progress:** check how things are developing and link back to the job definition and requirements.

This describes a continuous cycle of activity; indeed it may link back to a formal revision of your job description. Some of it is formal. The definition of the job, for instance, can result in a formal job description being issued. Some of it is informal, with development activity and evaluation both being made up, in part, of activity that is blended in with the ongoing job and with the regular dialogue between a manager and those they supervise.

The annual job appraisal (or indeed any additional scheduled meetings) is simply one part of this continuum. This view may help make the meeting seem a more routine and less exceptional activity. It also shows the necessity for follow-up action. Appraisal is not something that happens in isolation. It is part of a continuum and a catalyst to the whole process. Appraisal is concerned ultimately with prompting future performance and helping make it achieve results. So too are the actions that spring from it.

The system

A simple point first. Always complete any forms that link to appraisal promptly. First to comply with the system; it is a pity to blot your copybook as it were by missing the first deadline you have to hit after your appraisal meeting. Second, remember that if you do not deal with this sort of thing promptly your ability to recall salient details drops away fast (as anyone who has to compile minutes for meetings knows similarly). The details matter and you want there to be a clear record of what transpired.

If there are documents that will be sent to you by the appraiser ask when you will receive them. Link all documentation back to your appraisal collection file; the first actions to help make next year's appraisal go well take place immediately after this year's.

Link to your work system

Moreover, there may be a number of decisions and intentions to take further. You may have agreed to:

- check out suitable courses on a particular skill area and make suggestions as to what you should attend;

- provide additional background information about the past;

- take on new responsibilities that need briefing meetings to be set up;

- review targets or objectives more frequently in future, or for a period.

These and many more possible actions may need linking to your diary, confirming in memos and remembering for the future. Remember that if the manager who appraises you has numbers of people reporting to them, then they may collect a long list of follow-up actions. A suggestion that you document things where appropriate may make sure that it is remembered and that action follows sooner rather than later.

Some actions may be things you want to get out of the way, such as a further check on some aspect of your work that was questioned. Other actions may be things about which you are enthusiastic – they lead on to new chances or challenges. Follow up both, certainly, and maintain a positive attitude about the whole process.

Remember, feedback from you conditions future events. Say you obtain agreement to some form of training at your appraisal. You are keen to undertake it, follow up, schedule attendance on a course of some sort, and duly attend. If doing so is successful let your manager know – including a 'thank you' if appropriate – and link it back to the ongoing tasks. If it was not the right thing, say so. You may need to go on something else and others may be protected from a similar waste of time. The next chapter deals with training in more detail.

> **!** **ACTION:** There is always action of some sort to be taken after an appraisal – some immediate, some longer term. Never sideline this; deal with matters promptly to get the best from the event.

Future progress

Rome was not built in a day. And appraisals do not act to solve all problems and kick-start our progress, guaranteeing effortless generation of future results and rewards to match. But appraisals should be a constructive part of the continuity of consideration and action that links what we do now to the dynamic nature of the environment in which we work, and give us some hope of keeping up.

The appraisal meeting can be a significant part of the process. It will not automatically go well. Some systems are inflexible, inappropriate or ill thought out. Some managers regard the whole thing as a chore. Some aspects of corporate bureaucracy act to dilute the effectiveness of appraisals, maybe by focusing artificially on unconstructive aspects of them and forgetting the main purpose. Both appraisers and appraisees contribute to the process and either can act to ensure that it is constructive rather than irrelevant and time wasting.

If you play your part – working at it from one appraisal to the next – then you stimulate the process in the right direction. Small actions can make a significant difference, with just one extra, well-considered question taking the discussion into a new, helpful and relevant area. You have a good deal to gain; never let any aspect of your appraisal go by default.

Let's end this review of appraisal as it started by taking a strictly realistic view of the work environment. As has been said, the work environment is, in a word, dynamic. Jobs for life are a thing of the past and waiting for things to 'return to normal', some vision of more secure times, is simply not one of the options. Few, if any, people are paid just for turning up. All of us, at whatever level of the organizational hierarchy we work, are judged by results; that is fair – results are what we are there to achieve.

It is also reasonable that managers should want to know how people are doing and that they should seek to improve their performance. Individually most of us want that too. Job satisfaction comes, in large part, from a sense of achievement and we must know what, and how much, we are achieving. So appraisal is a practical tool in the management process. And ultimately its prime purpose is to increase the likelihood of *future* performance being satisfactory – better still of it qualifying as excellent.

Because you can get very close to what you do, the appraisal meeting represents a useful opportunity to step back and review how things are going, and to look ahead and plan how things can be made to go well in future. This is true of both the immediate job and how that reflects your longer term career intentions. Essentially, for those being appraised there are two key areas where appraisal can help; by:

- maximizing existing and future job performance;

- playing a part in longer term career planning and development (so the final check for you afterwards perhaps links to your career plan).

The two are clearly closely related. Careers tend not to prosper if performance in the current job is suspect. So any help that appraisal can give is to be welcomed in both respects. What did the old Beatles' song say? *I get by with a little help from my friends.* No one succeeds in a corporate environment entirely by their own efforts. Most of us benefit from a variety of advice, information and assistance along the way, which comes to us, wittingly or unwittingly given, from those with whom we work.

Appraisals – both the formal and informal type – should be seen in that light. Of course, there is an element of 'checking up' about the process, but it is – or should be – constructive, and a process that looks to the future. Ignore it or treat it lightly at your peril. See it as a resource that is part of what can help you succeed in job and career and then take an active view of getting the most from it; you will be able to make it do more for you.

The checklist below acts to sum up the key issues.

Example: taking a constructive approach to your appraisal

Specifically, you need to set yourself objectives under a number of headings:

- planning how to make positive points about performance during the period under review;

- being ready to respond to points raised, including negative ones, appropriately;

- projecting the right image;

- reviewing specific work plans for the next period ahead;

- reviewing factors on which success in the future depends;

- identifying the need or desirability for training and development;

- looking ahead to longer term career development;

- linking discussion to salary and benefits review.

The key to getting the most from appraisals can be summarized in 10 key points, as follows:

1. Take appraisal seriously (it is a luxury to be able to step back and think about what you are doing).

2. View it constructively – focus on what you (and your organization) can gain from it.

3. Study and become familiar with the system your organization uses.

4. Keep appraisals in mind during the year and gather the facts and information that will help your next one.

5. Prepare thoroughly for the meeting, thinking of what you want to discuss and anticipating what will be raised.

6. Aim to play an active part in the meeting, rather than simply be led by events.

7. Put your points over clearly and positively.

8. Ask anything where you feel comment or information would be helpful.

9. Record and action points agreed during the meeting (and be sure to hit any deadlines for action agreed).

10. Be open in discussion, constructive about criticism, positive about opportunities for the future and always receptive to new ways of doing things and new things you might do.

Although all appraisals may have to address strengths and weaknesses of performance, one that is simply unconstructive and from which nothing useful flows is just a waste of time. Company systems may demand that appraisals are gone through, perhaps for reasons of employment legislation, but if they are going to be done then the best should be gained from them. Of course this is dependent on both you and management; but make sure you play your part in making it constructive.

Finally, always keep your career plan firmly in mind throughout the process.

At the end of the day everyone wants to be successful. It is an old, but wise, maxim that there is a significant difference between five years' experience and one year's experience repeated five times. Ensuring that you are on the path towards five years' experience, and that your experience, competence, success – and thus your role – all grow, is a process that needs regular time and attention.

One repeating part of the process is your regular job appraisals: that is the annual appraisal and all the things that flow from it. Make the most of them and they can play a significant part in your progress and success.

6

The Development Process

It's what you learn after you know it all that counts.
— John Wooden

As the last two chapters have shown, appraisal relates very directly to development, although it is not the only prompt to making development take place. Be assured, progress in your career means being fit for the job now and also in terms of whatever you may do in future. Development is an ongoing process. It is possible to regard development as something that the organization, or your boss, does for you (occasionally). In that light it may sometimes be no great help, sometimes useful and sometimes spot on.

It is better to regard development as a personal responsibility, something that *you* make happen, rather than something that is wished on you; this is especially true if you want what is then done to assist your career short and long term rather than simply focus on your current role and responsibilities.

Thus self-development, as we might call it, implies a process directed at improvement: to assist you work better now, but with an eye on the future too. In a job context this in turn implies the aim of improving specific job performance and thus incorporating or extending the skills that make that possible. Much that has already been said suggests why such a process is necessary; here we examine something of the detail of how it can be made to happen. It needs more than some kind of 'good intention'. To be effective the process needs to be:

- consciously entered into;

- well planned;

- systematically executed;

- focused on clear objectives and intended to make a real and tangible difference.

Having said that, it should be acknowledged immediately that alongside the specific objectives there are – should be – more personal and intangible ones. One result of good self-development is that it can make your job more interesting, satisfying and fun. And it can also help your longer term career progress and help your overall advancement.

In a busy life an activity such as self-development must not be a chore, especially not an impossible one, so approaches to it must make it manageable. Certainly in today's work environment spending time on self-development is not a nice option – something to do a little of if time permits – it is a necessity. Your success and future prosperity depend on it; the only question is how much activity is necessary and what should this be?

The answer to this comes, in part, from an understanding and utilization of the development process.

The nature of the development process

This is the chapter in which the 'what you do' and 'how you do it' of self-development is examined. There is no magic formula, many different things can contribute to successful self-development and it is in deciding on the mix of what you do that you first influence your ultimate success.

Thinking about development

Remember that development can only ever do three things:

- *Impart knowledge:* so you can learn about whatever is necessary in your job from background knowledge to how your company's product works; both the span and depth of your knowledge matters.

- *Develop skills:* introducing you to new skills, maintaining, improving or refining your abilities in everything from core techniques in something like negotiation to specialist computer skills you may need to deploy.

- *Change attitudes:* study can change the way you think about things, although this may take longer than adopting some new skills. For example, something like managing your time effectively is as much a question of the attitude you take to it (and the habits this develops) as to slavishly following techniques.

Next, if your development is going to change anything, two other things are key:

- You have to set aside some *time* for self-development. This need not be excessive or unmanageable, but it needs to be there and it needs to be made available on a regular basis.

- *Application* is equally important. There is all the difference in the world between skimming through a book, to take a simple example, so that you can say that you have done so, and reading it carefully, studying it over a little longer period, making some notes and perhaps also resolving to take some action as a result.

In many jobs the evidence of results, whether good or bad, is clear. Although some development activity may stem from a more general 'look ahead', much of it will come from an examination of the current situation. Managers are charged with monitoring the performance of their staff, and the systematic way that they go about this can equally be applied to oneself.

Consider the formal process, mentioned earlier, first (how your manager might approach it with you in mind). The following stages can be identified:

- *Examine job description:* this allows you to review the levels of knowledge and skills that a particular *job* demands, and the attitudes required of the person who does it. This states the ideal and the current position and is not, at this stage, linked to the individual currently doing the job.

- *Examine the person:* this enables a look, alongside the ideal, at what the situation actually is currently. How do the knowledge, skills and attitudes of the individual stack up alongside what the job demands? This information comes from observation of the person, their performance and their results. Formal appraisal is a key part of this, as is other, less formal, evaluation.

- *Look to the future:* before reaching any conclusions from the process described so far, it is necessary also to think ahead, again focusing on the job rather than the individual. What will the job demand in future that will be different from the current situation? What developments – in the organization, in technology, in the market (affecting competition or the expectation of customers, for instance) and more – are coming? Specifically, what new skills, knowledge or attitudes will be necessary, and how will existing ones need to change?

- *Defining the gap:* together, two factors coming from the above may define a gap: the combination of any shortfall in current levels of competence plus the need to add to this for the future. This is the so-called *development (or training) gap* and describes the area towards which development must be directed with any individual.

Of course, the picture produced may be fine; no immediate action may be necessary. In so dynamic an environment, the reality at any particular moment is most likely that some action – major or minor – is, in fact, necessary. If so a plan of action is needed to deal with implementation. Again viewing this systematically provides a simple checklist approach as to what you need to do:

- *List what needs to be addressed:* whatever is identified, from minor matters that need only a small input to the development of new skills that must be approached from square one.

- *Rate the list in terms of priorities:* in most organizations, resources – that is time (including yours), money and training resources and facilities – are finite. It is unlikely to be possible to do everything that might be desirable instantly, and impossible to select what comes first or should be postponed without some clear thinking through of priorities.

- *Put some timing to it:* having established priorities you need to consider when things are to be done. What is urgent? What can be postponed without causing problems and what might be addressed in parts? (Perhaps with something being done early on, but action also planned to follow up and complete the training task later – something that might make it easier to sell to a manager).

- *Consider the most suitable method:* this factor needs to relate quite closely to timing. With a list of desirable development activities and priorities set, the next thing is to consider exactly how something will be approached (a course, a project, whatever).

- *Calculate costs:* this is always an important issue, and realistically may involve some compromise and a balancing of different approaches; when you are initiating things the question of who is to pay needs considering – you or the organization?

- *Link to an action plan:* the net result of these deliberations needs to be documented and turned into a rolling plan that sets out what will be done, in what way, when and who will be involved.

In this kind of way training and development activities can be considered, worked out and scheduled on a basis that makes sense. Such consideration must:

■ relate closely to operational matters;

■ link and liaise as necessary with any appropriate central department or manager (eg a training manager) – not least to draw on their experience and expertise; and

■ always, too, relate to your thoughts on career progression stemming from the analysis suggested in Chapter 3.

Something like this may happen to you, indeed the better your manager the more likely it is to happen.

> **!** **ACTION:** The personal implications are clear; whatever management may do, you need to think things through in a similar way and you need a written plan – one that you can roll forward and fine-tune over time. Starting from scratch this may take a moment; keeping it up to date and monitoring progress need not take long (the plan might well be one sheet of paper, though make sure what you write is sufficient to make sense when looked at some months on). The process is manageable; certainly it is wholly worthwhile in terms of the results you will get from it.

Development methods

Many ways of undertaking some self-development activity are possible. They range from reading a book (so, you are under way already!) to studying for a qualification; more details anon. Here we first consider the main approaches that you can take:

- *Activity that occurs:* a host of things go on day by day that are part of or linked to the development process. These include regular activities such as liaison with your manager, meetings and various kinds of evaluation including the ubiquitous annual job appraisal already reviewed. They also include more ad hoc activity: for example, you may occasionally attend a formal course. Two things are important here:

  - first, that you get the most from what goes on and integrate this into the totality of your overall development;

  - second, you may want to take action to prompt your manager or organization to take more such action, indeed to try to secure specific initiatives that you feel will help you now or in the future.

- *Your own activity:* this means activity that you instigate, personally and often privately. It might take advantage of company systems, say a library or resource centre, or it might utilize outside resources or simply be something you can do on your own or informally with others. *Note:* it is useful to establish things here as a habit, perhaps setting yourself a target, say to read a business book every month.

The task is to produce the best mix of activities you can that line up behind your own objectives. Some of these will certainly come in some way via your employer. (If not are they the right employer? Realistically, this is something you need to consider. Sometimes one needs to make a decision that your long-term future is not with your current employer.) Other activities will come only after some liaison or persuasion – deploying some of your communication skill internally – and more may be necessary on your own initiative. The reality will always be a mix of some sort. Certainly you should avoid your development being short of what is needed because your only approach is to accept and undertake what the organization makes available. It is your career and ultimately the responsibility for it going well is with you.

Positive results

Whatever activities you may undertake, and however they may be instigated, you want them to be useful. Overall there are four main ways in which development can help you:

■ *In your current job:* the first level of benefit is in your current job. Development can provide help, for example by strengthening or adding skills to your armoury, so that you can do it better. It can help you achieve better results – bearing in mind that even the best performance can be improved – and that in turn can be important to your future.

■ *In future jobs:* success in your current job can, of course, help you towards new ones. In addition, development may look ahead, focusing for example on skills that, although not essential in the short term, are a prerequisite for promotion. Development helps fit you for promotion and puts you in a better position to make a career move when you want.

■ *Increase your job rewards:* in some work (sales for example) rewards can be closely linked to success especially when success is not difficult to measure. In other jobs results may be more difficult to identify or tie down to an individual, although rewards may be linked to overall schemes such as profit-sharing arrangements. Remuneration is always best viewed as a package: salary, commission, expenses, car, pension arrangements, bonuses, share schemes and so on. Progress in your job, driven by development, helps secure you the returns you want both in your current job and as you progress in your career.

■ *Enhance your perception:* perception within an organization is important. It may have intangible elements to it, but it is something real – are you seen as successful, as a high flyer, as someone having abilities beyond your current responsibilities? Because of what development can do, its results can improve the perception of you that exists within (and outside) the organization. This is a not insignificant benefit and one worth bearing in mind.

Job performance plus job satisfaction

In addition, and of influence across the whole of your work and career, development influences job satisfaction. Whatever you want to do you probably want to enjoy it, to find it a challenge, to find it satisfying. However you define this for yourself, it is again worth bearing in mind. *You* make your career happen. Of course, many things influence it, but the job is to orchestrate the influences and make things go as far as possible the way you want. Aim high, and whatever else happens avoid being in a position where, if you pause to consider progress to date, your first comment begins *If only I had…*

> **!** **ACTION:** If you are to maximize your job performance, foster a successful career and make the progress you want, development, including that aspect of it on which you must be self-sufficient, is a vital activity. It is something to which you must take an active approach. It must reflect real life and it must reflect an objective view of things. You may have, or find you have, weaknesses that you need to work to correct. You may have particular skills that you must add to your capabilities for the future and certainly, like most of us, you probably have a continuing job to do just to keep up with the changing environment in which you work.

Remember the line, quoted earlier, from one of John Lennon's songs – 'Life is what happens while you are making other plans.' Time slips by all too fast and good intentions can remain just that. Development is not an option; it is a necessity. But it is something you can address and make successful and also something about which you should liaise with management (more of this later – see page 119). It helps you go where you want to go. In the next chapter we review a variety of methods that can help you move ahead.

7

Methods to Take You Forward

Knowledge advances by steps, and not by leaps.
— Lord Macauley

As a catalyst to improving or fine-tuning your competence, and hence benefiting your career, again there is merit in having a written plan; in this case it is one stemming directly from the analysis described in the last chapter and setting out your development goals. To complete this you need to consider *how* any training input you plan for yourself can be delivered. Even including consideration of methodology, the plan need not be voluminous. It might only be a couple of sheets of (A4) paper, perhaps with these linked to a simple year planner (the sort of thing that comes with a Filofax-style loose-leaf diary system is ideal). Alternatively, it might be a screen or two on your computer or electronic personal organizer, although this is personal information and needs to be kept private and easy to move on with you if necessary.

Whatever form it takes the plan can specify what you will do, when you will do it and the method(s) to be used.

Sometimes notes may be specific – *Attend presentation skills course 20/21 June* – on other occasions it may be only a guide, for example specifying that you will read a book on a particular subject – *during August*. For the first few months of the plan it should be more specific than it is likely to be further ahead; the planning process rolls on and things can be firmed up as time passes. You should use the plan to record the full implications involved. For instance, what do you want to do *after* attending a presentations skills course: make more presentations or get someone to critique the next one you make? Line up whatever sequence of events makes sense. If you ensure that when a moment is passed it records accurately what you did, then it will create a useful record.

Now, what are the options? What are the kinds of things that you can do and how do you decide what is best?

Reviewing and choosing methods

Perhaps the first thing to address here is some guidelines on assessing the relative merits of different methods. Without thinking about this in the right way, there is a danger that you will always select whatever seems 'easiest', and this may not give you the best results.

Choice of method must reflect, and sometimes be a compromise between, various criteria. These include what is most:

- *Effective* (and will be most likely to ensure that learning does take place).

- *Productive* (and will make the best use of time).

- *Convenient* (which includes what you are best set up to do, and how much something will disrupt operational matters – or not).

- *Interesting* (motivation is always an important side effect of development. It is something management should keep an eye on – certainly you will want to bear in mind making the process as stimulating as possible).

- *Timely* (in the sense of both when the development, or the result of it, is needed and in terms of fitting in with other operational considerations of timing – for instance, consider the seasonality of what you do; are there quiet times when a request to go on a course might be more likely to be agreed? Being seen to address something that will make for immediate improvement can usually do your profile no harm).

- *Fitting* (that is, what fits best into the continuum of other, and ongoing, training and development either that you plan or that you are required to do).

- *Well-tailored* (to what you want to achieve and the prevailing circumstances).

- *Financially suitable* (not necessarily the cheapest way of doing something, but always it must be possible to justify the costs – especially if you are financing it yourself). *Note:* if you regard the return as sufficiently important, although you may always want to start by asking your employer to fund any training you want to undertake, remember there may be some things worth personal expenditure. If you do this remember to keep records and receipts, as you may well be able to claim such costs against your tax.

Alongside all of the above is a fit with the topic; the topic may demand more or less in terms of what can realistically get you to grips with it. Choice of method has the overall intention of making the process both effective and productive. Some methods are not mutually exclusive and you may want to do a number of things in combination or in sequence, coming at something from a variety of directions. Smaller examples (if you can have a 'small' method) may act in their own right or be an inherent part of a larger event as, for example, reading a book may be useful before or after attending a course.

As has already been said, many ideas and approaches that qualify as methods are extremely simple. Others are more complex and time consuming, and realistically what is needed is a mix. Some examples follow; to start, we review the classic course – something that comes in a surprising variety of guises.

The traditional course (in all its forms)

There are all sorts of learning events and the terminology here is less than exact. There are courses, seminars, meetings, workshops, master classes, conferences and more. In considering what to use an assessment has to be made of the options.

You may be sent on courses, but you may also want to request attendance. Any course you pick must reflect your overall intentions and objectives (for job and career), then – our concern here – the question is which course to select? Answering this question is not a science, and judgement and preference play a key part. Some juggling of disparate factors may be necessary, and the following are designed to help cut through the plethora of alternatives with regard to the conventional course, and can assist sensible decision making:

- *How long?* Usually this is a compromise between what the content demands, the level of participation and the realism of time away from your job.

- *Internal or external?* Various factors are important here: would it be useful to get an outside perspective? To mix with others? What about timing? What internal resources exist? In a small organization there may be no option other than something external.

- *Which trainer?* You may feel a 'personality style' external event is best, or have preferences regarding which of a number of trainers or consultants you feel would be most useful.

- *What format?* Here there are many options, from a short session of a few hours to long courses; not least you must be realistic about how long you are likely to get agreement to be away from the job.

■ *How much participation?* This is not just a question of what would be most satisfying, but of what the topic needs, the number of participants and so on.

■ *The devil you know:* all things being equal, it may make sense to stick with a trainer or style of training that you have used in the past, and therefore know and like. This can lead to messages building progressively and logically one on another.

■ *Management preference:* here you need to consider what will be most likely to be approved – does the organization (or your boss) only like things that have an entirely practical focus or are they inclined to experiment?

Overall, there is another factor, always important, that of *cost*. Although poor training may be worse than none at all, one has to be realistic and cost is a factor that dictates, at least in part, what decisions to take. Again you need to be realistic; it might be better not to ask to go on a month's training three months into a new appointment, for instance.

Getting the best from course attendance

Whatever course is selected, you want to get the best from it. Two factors are important here:

■ *Pre-course briefing:* whether you have been involved in the choice to attend a particular course or not, you need to be clear why you are attending and what should come from it. It is well worth the few minutes it takes to sit down with someone – your own manager or a central training person – to go through this. You should be clear what the objectives of a course are, and its limitations – it may only address part of something you ultimately want to deal with comprehensively. Such a briefing will help you to go with clear and specific personal objectives in mind.

Such briefing and thinking sets up attendance so that its effectiveness is maximized. Most external consultants and training organizations are pleased to discuss pending or possible course attendance in this way, incidentally; if not, maybe they are not the best choice.

■   *Behaviour on the programme:* these days it is unlikely you will find yourself on a course you regard as useless. Even if you approach a course positively, however, you need to maximize the benefit of your attendance on it. After all, once it is over any action may be more difficult and, certainly on a short course, attention literally to the process of attending is worthwhile. So check out objectives, make a note of issues or problems you want to raise and generally think about how you can make attending a worthwhile experience (the next section explores this further).

Maximizing the benefit of attending courses

Some companies issue guidelines for those attending formal courses, whether external or internal. These may be useful to you and are worth studying for a moment. As an example, the boxed list that follows is one set of guidelines given to people attending public courses. This is adapted from my book *Improve your Coaching & Training Skills* (also published by Kogan Page). It certainly addresses some of the key issues and sets the scene for getting the most from the experience of attending.

NOTES FOR DELEGATES: an example of a document issued to delegates at the start of a course (or ahead of attendance)

1. This material contains all the basic details of this training programme. Further papers will be distributed progressively during the course so that a complete record will be available by the last session.

2. This is *your* seminar, and represents a chance to say what you think – so please do say it. Everyone can learn from the comments of others and the discussion it prompts.

3. Exchange of experience is as valuable as the formal lectures – but you need to *listen carefully* and try to understand other points of view if this is to work.

4. Do support your views with facts in discussion, use examples and stick to the point.

5. Keep questions and comments succinct – do not monopolize the proceedings, but let others have a say so that various view-points can be discussed.

6. Make points in context as they arise. Remember that partici-pation is an attitude of mind. It includes listening as well as speaking, but also certainly includes constructive disagree-ment where appropriate.

7. Make notes as the meeting progresses. There is notepaper provided in this binder. Formal notes will provide an aide-memoire of the content and coverage, so any additional notes should primarily link to your job and to action on your return to work. Even a few action points noted per session can act as a catalyst and help ensure action follows attendance.

8. A meeting with colleagues, staff or your manager on your return to normal working can be valuable, it acts as a bridge between ideas discussed here and action in the workplace and can make change more likely.

9. It will help everyone present if you wear your name badge, respect the Chair and the timetable, and keep mobile tele-phones and pagers switched off during the sessions.

10. This is an opportunity to step back from day-to-day operations and consider issues that can help make your job more effective. Be sceptical of your own operation, challenge ideas, remain open minded throughout and actively seek new thinking that can help you prompt change and improve performance.

Whether your organization produces something like this or not, these are sensible points and it is certainly always worth having such principles in mind when you attend any kind of formal session.

There may be other matters included also, such as the obligatory request to be politically correct in posing questions or giving examples. If you get such documentation and feel it leaves questions unanswered, do ask before or at the start of the course.

! **ACTION:** Attendance on courses demands more than passive acceptance. Think about what you may attend, what it will offer and how you will conduct yourself, make some notes and plan to get as much as possible from it.

Other forms of development

Activity courses

One special form of course is also worth a mention. Imagine: it is cold and wet, moorland stretches away into the mist and you know the nearest cup of tea and warm bath are miles distant. You and assorted colleagues are huddled under the dripping branches of a tree. On the ground nearby are three old car tyres, some lengths of rope, six planks of wood and a pink cushion. How do you turn all that into something that floats, cross the river and... but where actually is the river? The 'outward bound' type of course is loved and hated in equal measure.

Some people swear they are the ultimate developer of leadership skills or teamwork. Some just swear. Certainly their use needs care. Not every provider of such things is equally good; some are good at providing a physical challenge, but less good at relating it in any meaningful way to the workplace. Not every group is suited to this sort of thing, and certainly someone less physically able or adept might find tagging along after their more athletic teammates taught them nothing but resentment.

That said, they seem to suit the culture of some organizations and, if they do, they provide a different way of approaching certain training tasks. They are almost certain to get the undivided attention of the group for a while; it is pretty difficult to worry about immediate operational problems when you are high in the air dangling on the end of a rope over mud of indeterminate depth. They can be fun but, if you find yourself going on one, the question of briefing and exactly what management expect you to get from it is doubly important. If this is not clear in any way, always ask – and ask before you are wet, muddy and wondering what is going on!

Simulations

Almost at the other end of the spectrum of training methods from activity courses, simulations focus attention very specifically on one area of activity. Their teaching is through involvement, often with technology lending a hand. Typically a computer program provides the basis to experiment with complex interactions.

For example, there are simulations used in marketing training. They set up a market situation: products, prices, people, markets, competitors and more. Decision making can be input and not only recorded, but also recorded in such a way that the whole complex web of 'given' factors changes. Thus a decision to raise a product's price will see volume sold and profitability adjust accordingly; and competition takes action in response also. Some such training devices are for individuals to use, others work – sometimes competitively – with a group of people participating together.

Simulations can provide considerable realism and considerable stimulation. They tend not to be suitable as a first exposure to a topic, relying as they do on the participants having some knowledge of the subject. They need clear briefing and, sometimes, preparatory work to set them up, but this is understandable given their role and purpose.

If you want to check out this sort of thing, a good example is a marketing training device called *Markstrat*. The organization producing this, and it is one that has been around a while and is tried and tested, is Stratx Simulations; if you check their website it will give you a flavour of how this sort of thing works: (www.stratxsimulations.com).

Packaged training

This term is usually used to describe training resources with two characteristics. First, they use a variety of aids to package their training, including audio and video material, programmed learning texts and, of course, computer-based training (often shortened to CBT) particularly using CDs, DVDs and so on. Second, they are designed to be worked on a, sometimes largely unsupervised, solo basis or, if with a group, through 'facilitation' (someone to lead the way through, rather than a fully fledged trainer).

The simplest form will set participants off down a road involving a number of elements. For instance, you may work through a work-book, which leads the process. This will have you pause on occasion as you do so: to view video clips, listen to audio elements, and answer questions (which with programmed learning devices can redirect you, recapping if knowledge is not proven to be at a certain level) or, where group work is involved, to interact with others.

You can find good things in this sort of format; if so then you may find them in libraries or be able to persuade your company to finance them (pointing out that they are then a permanent asset and that once you have used them other people can do so too). Much that is packaged is now also computerized.

Open learning

This phrase is used to encapsulate a number of techniques linking work done 'at your desk' to a central point elsewhere (often now via the internet) that coordinates the activity (hence the alternative description of distance learning). This has become a popular way of handling the load of studying for some sort of qualification – where exercises, projects and such like are set and marked by tutors at the body offering the course. Study may involve all sorts of mixtures of method, from reading to watching videos provided and, of course, computer work (some now online, some even able to be organized on a team basis).

The principle is also used for job-based training and an open learning set-up may exist in a large organization where staff work in many widely spread locations.

Resource centres

These are often the preserve of larger companies. The idea developed from the simple library and that element remains. Beyond that, however, the resource centre has a range of developmental materials and any equipment they demand. Here someone can go and watch a video, spend time at a dedicated computer learning station, engage in certain small group activities – or just find a helpful book or a word of advice.

There is no one definition of a resource centre. Different organizations configure them differently, and of course they change over time. Not only do they provide an aid to learning, their very existence contributes to the creation of a development culture, demonstrates that development is important and helps both managers and staff fit undertaking it into a busy life.

Job rotation and swapping

There are a variety of ways to incorporate development into the everyday work of the organization. Sometimes this is simply a matter of change. People are intentionally moved into new jobs, rather different to what they were doing previously, for developmental reasons. There is a domino effect as people move round and the effect can thus affect many people. I deal with some organizations where this is an established pattern: no one expects to stay in the same post for more than a short number of years. Not only is this seen as aiding the development of the individuals concerned, it is regarded as stimulating the new thinking and new ideas necessary to prevent the organization from becoming struck in a rut. It also may benefit staff retention (people are less likely to leave through boredom). This may or may not be something your employer does as a routine (if it is, you may want to aim to influence how it affects you) but there is no reason why you cannot make suggestions even about a one-off idea.

Films

Training films cover a range of topics well, especially personal skills ranging from selling and negotiating to time management, and all the major providers have catalogues and websites you can check out. Films do not offer complete training in a moment – that would be unrealistic – but they do offer good encapsulations of principles and illustrate matters in a memorable way (or the good ones do). They are quite expensive to buy or even to hire, but you can make suggestions about using them at meetings (so that costs can be spread over a number of people), look at them in a resource centre if you have one or attend the previews that seem to be regularly scheduled for assessment purposes. The manuals that accompany such films are usually useful too.

Secondment

For some companies a good, and convenient, way of developing people is to post them for longer or shorter periods away from their present location. This may simply be to a branch office (or from a branch to HQ). Or to a location where activity is specialized: a research facility perhaps.

For multinationals and others involved in business internationally, the tactic may typically involve overseas postings (or indeed job rotation). Myles Proudfoot of Proctor & Gamble, mentioned on page 33, is evidence of this. In his case, the thinking was certainly that such moves will allow him to acquire experience and may jump him up the corporate hierarchy faster than continuing to work in his home base would have done.

Some policy and guidelines for those seeking such opportunities may exist in a large organization (I doubt if it is a novel occurrence in such as P & G, above). In other circumstances it is again something to consider and suggest; although it may need a persuasive case to be made for it.

There are various opportunities here, not all limited to large multinationals. For example, secondment may be arranged:

- in a different division of an organization;

- in a subsidiary company;

- with a customer (or supplier) organization;

- with the organization of an agent or distributor;

- with a professional body (some of which are supported by their member companies seconding staff to them for a while; usually where there is reciprocal benefit).

It could be round the corner, up three flights of stairs or thousands of miles away. You may well be able to think of, or use, other forms of secondment. Swaps – exchanges – are possible also, organized so that two people, and both organizational parties, benefit. This kind of arrangement might be essentially short term, say a week in the Paris office. Or, more relevant in this chapter, it might mean swapping roles and locations for a year or more.

Sabbaticals

Here is something that will perhaps be regarded as something of a luxury. But it can have real value, and be cost effective too. It can take various forms, but in one company I worked with, one category of senior people were allowed to take three months' (paid) leave (in addition to normal holidays) after working with the company for 15 years. In consultancy – a fee-earning and time-dependent business – this represented a significant cost. Equally it was a business in which many did not habitually take long holidays because of the nature of the business, so in some ways the time was, in part, a quid pro quo.

Certainly it was highly motivational, both to those in the prescribed category and to those who aspired to be. I cannot now remember whether it was compulsory to do so, but such extended periods of leave often included a project, something to which no time would otherwise be given. For example, travel was one thing people sometimes wanted to do, and this linked usefully to the international development of the business, allowing more leisurely research and investigation than might otherwise have occurred. If this was coupled with some fee-earning work it made good sense all round.

There are a number of variables here, certainly the:

- duration selected;

- number and level of staff to be involved;

- purpose (or lack of it) given to the gap period;

- reporting back, if appropriate.

One can think of all sorts of things this system could be used for, and one is certainly development. This is something else to seek out or suggest, perhaps.

No stone unturned

A complete list of methods is neither possible here nor is it intended (though the next chapter adds other possibilities of a different nature). Indeed the inventive person will see any list they compile expanding as time goes by.

It is worth putting yourself in a position to check, quickly and regularly what is possible, what is new and what else you can do. Thus it may also be worthwhile to:

- subscribe to various trade and business journals, and those specific to the function and role in which you work;

- subscribe also to relevant newsletters, e-zines and suchlike delivered automatically to your computer;

- allow your name to be added to certain mailing lists (for instance to get news of the latest products produced by a training film company whose preview meetings you might attend);

- occasionally (regularly?) attend relevant exhibitions (for example a trade show to improve competitor intelligence or a training exhibition to see what new development aids might be available and useful); ditto trade or functional conferences;

■ cultivate a friend in the HR department (or similar) especially if you are in a large organization; or indeed anyone else for that matter who gives access to useful information.

All activity designed to make you more effective in your job and to boost your 'career fitness' is an open-ended process.

> **ACTION:** Consider the options here carefully. Some things can be adopted on a regular basis, undertaking them can become a positive habit. Other things are more occasional, or one-off, and everything must be assessed regularly to see if it is still useful or if your mix of development activity should contain something else instead.

The next chapter looks at further details about methods, and illustrates more about how things work and what works best.

8

Creating Career-Enhancing Opportunities

You grab a challenge, act on it, then honestly reflect on why your actions worked or didn't. You learn from it and then move on. That continuing process of lifelong learning helps enormously in a rapidly changing economic environment.
— John Kotter, academic at Harvard Business School

A plethora of development methods was touched on in the last chapter, and the point was made that everything needs to be considered in light of clear intentions and objectives.

Making it work

With that still in mind we now look at how this sort of approach can work for you. The methods and examples selected are chosen, not to be comprehensive, rather to illustrate the mix of activities that can be used, either taken advantage of or prompted, and the manageability and effectiveness of such a mix.

Obtaining constructive feedback

The first thing to concentrate on that allows regular and useful self-improvement is feedback. Where does this come from? Essentially there are three sources:

1.   *Your manager:* feedback will in all probability be offered from your manager and a formal and ongoing system of working practice needs to be developed between the two of you (see next main heading). Beyond that, remember that it is as much for you to suggest things as wait for them to be offered and that even the simple principle of asking questions can provide a great deal of information. Suggest understates the matter. Realistically, you often have to sell ideas to a manager – and that means that you must find reasons why they will want to say yes (benefits to them) – rather than just say something beginning with *I want...* Indeed, such an 'I want' list of reasons is the worst possible way to try to persuade anyone.

2.   *Your colleagues:* this category includes your peers, those working at a similar level or in a similar way to you, or other people with whom you can share experience if your respective work means that you might learn something from each other. It also includes others around your organization; some, such as the training manager, have already been mentioned.

3.   *Your work contacts:* that is, those with whom your work involves you – this might include people inside the organization, in other departments or functions, or outside, for example customers, suppliers or collaborators. Your experience with these should provide you with endless feedback just through observation. Ask yourself: *what did I say and do, how did I do it and what was the reaction?* Note – honestly – the facts and resolve to learn from them. But you can do more than this; you can ask them – carefully, selecting those most likely to be prepared to welcome this kind of exchange, and without saying *Aren't I just the best person you have ever met?* The thing to test here is not how you work directly – *what did you think of the questions I asked in that meeting?* – but rather reactions. For example, you can ask about your communicating skill. Did you make something clear? Were questions left unanswered? Were you suitably persuasive, if necessary? Did you negotiate the best deal? The answers to such questions are always useful. Sometimes answers can be surprising. For example, I have regularly talked to salespeople who have had to adapt their approach to take up less time with customers, although it only became clear as a

result of specific questions; previously the customers had been polite enough to say nothing.

What you are looking for here are two things:

- *Signs of weakness:* what do you do that could in some way be done better? It pays to adopt a positive and constructive attitude to criticism. It is very easy to allow an instinctive defensive reaction to blind you to lessons that can be useful. In any case, most often you are not going to be told you are total rubbish, and may only need to make minor adjustments to ensure that something is significantly improved in future.

- *Strengths:* it is just as important to discover what goes well. This is not simply so that you can pat yourself on the back (though a little self-motivation does no harm), it is again so that you can fine-tune your approach. Ask yourself how you can build on strengths, where you can use something more or in different ways. Again this kind of process is a sure path to improved performance.

Putting feedback to work

To make any activity of this sort work you need a clear idea of the areas on which you should focus. At one level it is easy; for example, to return to the idea of presentations commented on earlier, ask:

- How did you start a presentation?

- How quickly did you establish a rapport?

- How clearly and thoroughly did you make its purpose clear?

- Was the case you made clear, attractive and credible?

- How well did you describe matters: was it understandable, even memorable?

But such a list only highlights the classic stages of a presentation. You may want to focus on more, including:

■   how well you prepared;

■   your time management (finishing on time is always appreciated);

■   use of visual aids;

■   pace and variety of delivery;

■   management and direction of the overall talk;

■   parting impression;

■   follow-up action;

■   display of empathy.

You can doubtless extend and personalize this sort of list. For example, you may want to monitor your powers of description (I loved a description that I think I heard on BBC radio: someone described something as being as slippery as a freshly buttered ice rink. Now that really *is* slippery). Language can be a powerful tool. Or you may want to focus on how you encapsulate what you have to say within a specific amount of time – and more.

> **!** **ACTION:** Much of what needs to be done here is made easier by habit. Some people seem to emerge from every meeting they conduct, or project in which they are involved with having something to carry forward and which they can use to assist them in the future; it makes sense to work actively to establish such a habit.

Getting others to help you is useful too.

Getting the most from management

Most people reading this will have a manager, even in a small organization. Even if you have not, read on and bear in mind what is said here later when we review mentoring. Three particular ways of interacting with your manager are worth thinking about:

- *Ongoing counselling (usually involving evaluation and a link to development of all sorts):* most managers will evaluate what any member of their team is doing and what results they are getting. Whereas a bad manager may see this as just looking at the figures and shouting when targets are missed, many see this role more constructively. They take the view that even the best performance can be improved and act to do just that. This may involve simple discussion or observation (again, presentation is a good example, but so too in a different way is report writing). Observation can seem intrusive, but remember it is the *only* way in which they can observe and investigate *how* you do things (sitting at their desk they can only see the figures or second-hand reports that emanate from what you do). So this is something to be approached constructively. Take on board what they say, ask questions, try things out on them and use them as a sounding board. Many tasks are carried out pretty much solo – make use of time spent to analyse and help take your approaches and skills forward. This is a specific form of what is more generally called 'training-on-the-job'. *Note:* if you decide on and suggest the timing of such observation and exchanges it may avoid awkward moments being picked by chance and make such encounters more useful.

- *(Departmental) meetings:* every so often a team will get together; this may be weekly, monthly, whatever, with the frequency dependent on such factors as cost and geography as well as the kind of job the team does. However often this happens you want to get the most from it. Again, a good manager will see this as an opportunity to inform, motivate, gather and exchange ideas – and undertake development activities. It is sometimes a problem to keep regular meetings fresh, indeed they can settle into a repetitive format and a bit of a rut. So do not be backward in making suggestions or volunteering to initiate action in this area (you might collaborate with colleagues in so doing – *a number of us think...*). A number of things are possible:

- *Training games and exercises:* these are designed to focus attention on one particular aspect of the job. They might include something as simple as a quiz to check knowledge, through to elaborate, often team-based, exercises.

- *Role playing:* this is a classic way of experimenting with an interactive skill such as selling, interviewing, negotiating or conducting or participating in meetings. Simple versions of it can be used in just a few minutes in a meeting (see box).

Example: role playing

Formal role play can be an inherent part of a training session or course. It may involve using audio or video equipment to record the role play so that replaying it can form the basis of a more detailed critique designed to lead to change. Equally, it can be used much less formally in any kind of group meeting. For example, at a sales meeting so-called carousel role play might be used (where two people start a conversation – in this case between buyer and seller – and then two others take over the roles and run the conversation on; it can thus involve a whole group very quickly and create a complete conversation for analysis).

Although role play is a tried and tested technique and there is no reason for it not to work well, it does need some care. Certainly there are things that can jeopardize its success. Be careful of potential dangers including:

- over-awareness of the camera (where what happens is recorded for critique);

- overacting to the camera, indeed a belief that role play demands 'acting';

- the difficulty of being 'on show' in front of peers;

- poor role play briefs (ask if you are not sure what you are trying to do);

- incomplete or unconstructive feedback after the role play is complete (again ask);

- those watching feeling excluded (ask for or suggest an observer role).

Such techniques can be used in many ways and areas of work. Viewed positively, role play can be organized to avoid the above hazards and can achieve one or more of the following:

- reproduce real life as closely as possible;

- allow practice of important, difficult or unusual situations;

- introduce and practise a skill new to people;

- develop confidence;

- experiment with new approaches;

- change negative habits or reinforce positive ones;

- reinforce knowledge and instil useful reflexes;

- utilize analytical skills (used in the feedback and critique).

All these are things you should recognize as being worthwhile. Role play offers a safe environment. It may be a touch awkward to role play in front of colleagues, but it is much better to practise and experiment with new ideas in this way before risking all in a real situation.

- *Brainstorming:* as a route to generating ideas this can work well (although it needs to be properly set up and carried out – see example in the following box – it can also be instigated informally amongst a group of like-minded colleagues).

Example: brainstorming for success

Brainstorming is a group activity and can be used to provide an almost instant burst of idea generation. Working with a group of people (maybe three or four up to a dozen works most easily) it needs a prescribed approach, thus:

- gather people around and explain the objectives (clearly everyone wants to know what exactly it is that ideas are required about and why);

- explain that there are to be *no comments* on ideas at this stage;

- allow a little time for thought (singly or, say, in pairs);

- start taking contributions and noting them down (publicly on, say, a flipchart);

- when a good-sized list is established and recorded, then analysis can begin;

- grouping similar ideas together can make the list more manageable;

- open-minded discussion can then review the list;

- identify ideas that can be taken forward.

Such a session must exclude the word 'impossible' from the conversation, at least initially (and especially when used in senses such as *It's impossible, we don't do things that way* (why not?); or *It's impossible, we tried it once and it didn't work* (how long ago and in what form?).

By avoiding any negative or censorious first responses, by allowing one idea to spark another and variations on a theme to refine a point (perhaps taking it from something wild to something practical), a brainstorming session can produce genuinely new approaches.

It can be fun to do, satisfying in outcome and time-efficient to undertake – and members of a group who brainstorm regularly get better at it, and quicker and more certain in their production of good, useable ideas. It is something to suggest perhaps, as well as to participate in, however it occurs.

■   *Job performance appraisal* (the classic 'annual' appraisal): the point has been made about taking a constructive approach to various systems and processes within the organization. None have such wide-ranging influence as the (annual) job appraisal. You have to resolve and act to get the most from it. A useful (rather than a 'good') appraisal:

- focuses your thinking, and your subsequent development plan, on areas that need attention – that is both strengths and weaknesses;

- provides immediate feedback and counselling, which can be useful;

- gives you the opportunity to make suggestions regarding company-sponsored development activity;

- sets up actual development activities that can form the core of your own, perhaps more extensive, plan.

These points focus on the development side of appraisal. It is also an opportunity to project the right image, consider long-term career development and, not least, to link to the specific job to be done over the coming year. A good manager will always take a constructive view of appraisal; realistically it is something that some companies organize less than perfectly and which some managers find awkward to do. It certainly warrants your taking a suitable initiative to help ensure it is as useful for you as possible.

Remember too that an appraisal meeting is not a one-off event, it may well – indeed should – link to other conversations of various sorts throughout the year, and you need to get the most from these as well. This was reviewed in detail in Chapters 4 and 5.

All in all, your manager (well, a good one) is the best resource you are likely to have available regularly to assist your development. Not only should they help in the way that they work with you, but they should also make possible other things that are then implemented on your own – for instance in the training they allow or instigate.

Making it happen

A host of developmental things can be done and made to work if you think constructively and broadly about fitting them into the day-to-day work. For example:

- In one financial services organization, certain jobs routinely involved making formal 'on-your-feet' presentations. These were important and needed to be well executed. In addition to undergoing training people needed practice. At the suggestion of one team member certain internal meetings adopted a rule that anyone making a significant contribution had to stand up to do so. Effectively, this increased the number of presentations people made and provided an opportunity for comment and critique, which assisted the way skills were developed.

- In a publishing company one salesperson told me that she made a point of observing certain competitive salespeople (with much selling taking place in open areas of bookshops, a little judicious browsing made this easy to do). 'Both what they do, and how buyers react, lead to good ideas and allows me to make positive adjustments to my approach,' she said. Good idea, and a number of industries and jobs work in a way that allows this sort of thing to be done.

- In several companies I know there is a mandatory requirement for written documents going to customers (reports and proposals) to be read by someone other than the writer before they are sent. This is essentially a check, but people learn from it too.

Making the most of circumstances

Productivity is important, but so too is relaxation; all work and no play makes Jack a dull boy as the saying has it. So at this stage it should be recognized that the overall intention here is to put together an appropriate and manageable mix of development and career-building activity, not to unreasonably utilize every waking moment. That said, you should at least consider the way you work and see what possibilities this suggests. Two linked examples may help to make the point:

- *Car audio:* how far do you drive each year? More apposite still given today's traffic conditions, how long do you spend in the car? Some of that time could be spent doing something useful (and be safer than talking on a mobile phone). Virtually all cars have a CD player in them and a wealth of useful material is available in this form, specifically:

  - some companies issue newsletters, product briefings or training in this form; a variety of training packages are available for purchase in this form too;

  - a variety of business books are available in audio form.

Time spent listening to such material can be useful, interesting and stress busting (making you forget that traffic jam about which you can do nothing) – it can provide a constructive moment or a long-term project (for example, you could learn a language).

- *Other journeys:* although the above is stated in terms of a car journey, if you commute by train or have regular flights you also have the opportunity to listen to something (other than music) on say an iPod or similar. Indeed the range of gadgets that make this sort of thing possible increase as you watch; maybe you are reading this book on an electronic device such as the Sony Reader or Amazon's Kindle.

Development circles

Some years ago the Japanese began using a technique, taken up around the world in various ways, called quality circles. The idea was that a continuous focus could be kept on quality (primarily in a factory and production context) and a flow of ideas generated, the best of which could be taken up, implemented and used to produce productivity increase. Circles, groups of people of a size enabling easy discussion, were set up. Over time they looked at a whole series of issues (eg something with a specific description such as reducing waste of raw materials in a particular phase of production) and essentially brainstormed the matter. Ideas were fed up the organization, through a hierarchy of groups, the best and most practical being approved by management and implemented into operations. Communication was organized to be two-way so that everyone knew what was being achieved.

The basic principle of a permanent, or semi-permanent, organization of people focused on improvements has been copied and modified and made to work usefully in many different contexts since the idea of quality circles originated. Another area on which a similar approach has been used successfully is that of customer service, for example.

This sort of procedure can, like brainstorming on its own, produce learning in the area of creativity. Arranged with this sort of formality it can also direct people towards a whole range of other useful skills. For example:

■ Someone has to chair the sessions.

■ People have to listen and contribute.

■ Matters have to be reported back up the line, reports written and presentations made. An element of competition and incentive can be used to add to peoples' concentration (a bonus payment for the team producing the most valuable idea, perhaps).

Thus such a scheme can be used overtly or otherwise to progress a variety of development aims with some of these skills in mind; it is a good example of development and operational activity being progressed usefully alongside each other so that both gain.

Useful people

Many different people may be able to help in your plans to become and stay career fit. We will start with comment about one resource everyone but the self-employed has and which can certainly assist development – your boss.

The learning manager

If the term 'learning organization' can be used (it is: it means one that encourages ongoing learning and acts to make it possible), then the term learning manager makes similar sense. Surveys show that at the very top of the qualities that people look for in a boss are that they are 'someone I learn from'. A good manager can be your single most important spur to development. (If yours is the very reverse then it needs thinking about: are you going to succeed in such a circumstance? It may affect your future.) A good manager will consider development important, they will recognize that it serves a positive purpose (not just addressing weaknesses), and will work with their people to identify and close any development gap.

Realistically, you thus have two routes to obtaining assistance from your manager:

- taking advantage of the things they offer;

- encouraging – and sometimes persuading – them to do more or let you do more.

Your manager stands or falls on your performance, and that of others who report to them. They have a vested interest in your doing well and in helping you do just that. Whatever your role, there are certainly things that should happen and which you can use to your developmental advantage – both things that occur or which you might prompt in some way.

Whatever you may learn from your own manager, there are other people who can help too. Some can do so on a regular basis and this creates an invaluable process called mentoring.

Volunteering

It used to be a famous military expression that one should 'never volunteer for anything'. In context here it can be useful; although sensibly used with care. Given what you are trying to achieve, work out what actions and involvements might be helpful, either to learning and accelerating experience or to actually help jump you ahead. With that in mind maybe you should volunteer to:

- join a committee;

- take on a project;

- carry out external duties (attending a trade function of some sort, perhaps);

- take over something for your manager (maybe even something tedious: writing a report for them if you need the practice or if it will usefully put your name on it);

- help induct or brief newcomers;

- investigate some possible new opportunity or methodology.

There is much to consider here, and although you do not want to collect a long list of things that take time away from priorities, some may well help both in terms of what you will do and who you will meet. Being prepared to take on some things may put you in a good light as well; however, avoid what I call 'black hole' jobs that are ridiculously time consuming and will always upset someone (such as planning the company's anniversary celebrations, perhaps).

Mentoring

A mentor is someone who exercises a low-key and informal developmental role. More than one person can be involved in the mentoring of a single individual and, although what they do is akin to some of the things a line manager should do, more typically in terms of how the word is used a mentor is specifically *not* your line manager. It might be someone more senior, someone on the same level or from elsewhere in the organization. An effective mentor can be a powerful force in your development. So how do you get yourself a mentor?

In some organizations this is a regular part of ongoing development. You may be allocated one or able to request one. Equally you may need to act to create a mentoring relationship for yourself (something else that may demand persuasion). You can suggest it to your manager, or direct to someone you think might undertake the role, and take the initiative.

What makes a good mentor? The person must:

- have authority (this might mean they were senior, or just that they were capable and confident);

- have suitable knowledge and experience, counselling skills and appropriate clout;

- be willing to spend some time with you (their doing this with others may be a positive sign).

Finding that time may be a challenge. One way to minimize that problem is to organize mentoring on a swap basis: someone agrees to help you and you line up your own manager (or you for that matter) to help them, or one of their people.

Then a series of informal meetings can result, together creating a thread of activity through the operational activity. These meetings need an agenda (or at least an informal one), but more important they need to be constructive. If they are, then one thing will naturally lead to another and a variety of occasions can be utilized to maintain the dialogue. A meeting – followed by a brief encounter as people pass on the stairs – a project and a promise to spend a moment on feedback – an e-mail or two passing in different directions – all may contribute. What makes this process useful is the commitment and quality of the mentor. Where such relationships can be set up, and where they work well, they add a powerful dimension to the ongoing cycle of development, one that it is difficult to imagine being bettered in any other way.

Overall, what you learn from the ongoing interactions and communications you have with your line manager and others can be invaluable. It may leave some matters to be coped with in other ways, but it can prove the best way to cope with many matters and also to add useful reinforcement in areas of development that also need a more formal approach. As both parties become familiar with the arrangement, and with each other, it can become highly productive. Having been lucky enough to have someone in this role myself for many years I well know that often just a few minutes spent together can crack a problem or lead to a new initiative.

Note: a mentor is usually taken to be someone senior to the person to whom they act as mentor. But a similar relationship is possible with a colleague (for example, other members of your team or department). There is no reason why you cannot forge a number of useful and reciprocal alliances, perhaps each designed to help in rather different ways.

This is often an underrated methodology and well worth investigating, experimenting with and using. The example in the following box is particularly relevant to career change.

Mentoring in action

As an example of informal mentoring – unconnected to any organization structure – enhancing a career, let me introduce you to another consultant, Frances Kay. Frances contacted me a few years ago saying in effect 'You've written lots of books, can you show me how to get published?' Fair question, books not only generate revenue for an author, but in the business area if the author does allied work then the visibility they can also create can produce requests for other things – training and so on. We scheduled a kind of tutorial session; indeed I think I was paid for doing this. In this I reviewed the process, ways of working with publishers and more. Subsequently, after more discussion and liaison, I was able to match her to a publisher, and in due course Frances's first book was published.

Because we got on well we have met since on a regular basis. To begin with this was primarily to extend the opportunity for Frances to pick my brains, but mentoring, particularly if, as in this case, those involved become friends, works best in the long term when it becomes two-way. Now what we do is probably better described as networking and involves some tangible collaboration too: in 2009 we co-authored the book *Tough Tactics for Tough Times* (Kogan Page), about surviving the recession; indeed we have worked together in a number of ways that have been interesting, profitable and – this matters too – fun.

The point of quoting this is that it is an example of classic career management and development. Frances wanted to add book writing to her consulting portfolio of work, in part, as I have said, because of the visibility it can afford. It could, she believed, change her work pattern, producing more income from work done at home and reducing the amount of time she spent with clients and in travelling. It could also be useful promotionally. She recognized that some assistance might get her started in this new, though allied, field more easily than going it alone. Indeed she recognized that a learning curve was involved. The action she took was designed to accelerate her experience and promptly move forward her change of work portfolio.

Some time on, this has been very successful. At the last count she has had 20 titles published, worked with a number of publishers, and continued to collaborate with both others and me. She has produced what for me is certainly the best book around on networking, *Successful Networking*, and, working with Nielsen Kite to produce what is the only book on Neuro Linguistic Programming that has ever made sense to me, the very practical *Understanding NLP: Strategies for better workplace communication without the jargon* (Kogan Page).

This seems to me to demonstrate very well the process of moving forward in a career. New skills and processes were involved here and getting to grips with them had to precede getting into a new area of work to make it possible. Whatever the circumstances

---

– you may want to take on new tasks, new responsibilities; whether to enhance your existing job or better fit you for another involving an upward step – such action may be necessary. Whatever that involves, and mentoring or training are just two possible actions, setting things up right makes sense and makes success both more likely and likely to be possible sooner than would an ad hoc approach.

Certainly it worked for Frances and for me; I have learnt a good deal from the interaction, too, and have enjoyed the experience. What is more I have no hesitation in recommending what she has done to those seeking guidance on the topics about which she writes. Keep her name in mind when you choose a business book.

Networking

Networking is a well-established process these days. As the old saying has it, 'It is not what you know, it is who you know that matters.' Networking can assist business directly, it can assist career progress – and it can assist learning. All of which seems to make it a must in context here.

Your line manager and anyone in a mentoring role are obviously prime contacts. Beyond that you should keep in touch with people, other than your manager, who may be able to assist your development. There may be a variety of them. They may include: your manager's manager, a company training manager and others in Human Resources (HR), the Personnel Manager, Technical people (if you work in an organization with technical products your product knowledge may be improved simply by meeting regularly and informally with a contact in a technical role), and whoever may run any resource centre the company may maintain.

The other key liaison to run is with colleagues. If you work in a large organization people may be separated geographically; however, contact may still be possible, if only by e-mail, and may well be useful, extending the network of people who can help. Networking may be useful simply at the level of having a sounding board, and a companion for lunch. Differences of experience, skill or outlook could make it much more creative and see it result in very direct career boosting. As an example of the wide range of possibilities here, the box that follows looks at an international dimension of self-development. You may well want to organize, and interact with, an international network of contacts. Ask questions – *Do you have anyone in the office there that knows about X?* – work from one person to the next and keep in touch with those that seem, or prove, useful.

Networking example: international possibilities

If you have an international element to your job this may act to direct what you might do. Even if not, there may still be merit in looking further afield. Start at home as it were and work your way out. Make use of links that exist even if you are not involved in them. If your company has an office, a distributor or other contacts or arrangements in a foreign city get the contact name. This might not be the one you ultimately want but they may lead you to it.

Perhaps I can illustrate this principle with a personal example. I work regularly in South East Asia. One contact I have established in Singapore is a local consultant called Gary Lim, and this relationship provides a classic example of long-distance networking. Of course, we meet occasionally (not least, he's an excellent guide to local eating!), but more often contact is via e-mail and the occasional posted item.

Through him I can:

- obtain support and assistance of many sorts (for example, he once got a prompt cheque from what looked like being a bad debtor in Singapore by making a single phone call);

- extend my range of contacts by linking to others he knows;

- check the local view on something (economic, cultural or whatever);

- find a sounding board for ideas or to check something factual;

> ▪ discover other sources of information and advice (from a local library to a website in China).
>
> And more besides; and many of these contacts I learn from. It is also an interesting and pleasant contact – he's a nice guy! As I said to another colleague the other day 'Everyone should have a Gary in every overseas location that's important to them.' I hope he finds his link with me useful also.

Of course the people you link up with need to be tailored to your situation and your needs. Remember, networking is a two-way process, you get out what you put in, but it is also a very constructive one and should be part of anyone's career building and self-development activity.

Qualifications

Whatever your age or stage in your career and whatever your existing level of qualifications, consideration of your circumstances could indicate that further qualifications are worth acquiring and could assist your future career. There are routes to a variety of qualifications that may act to assist different careers. Their advantages are essentially threefold. First, study can include content that directly assists with what you need to know and be able to do in order to do either your current, or some future, job. Second, they may not just be useful in enabling you to do a job well, but instrumental in allowing you to qualify for, and be appointed to, a new job. In the second case the fact of studying for, or having passed, some qualification is as important to the situation as the actual practical value of what is learnt. Indeed, the way in which such things enhance your image is certainly a specific consideration. Third, there is the process of undertaking such things. Study may be in a variety of forms, including part-time courses and distance learning. But most represent an opportunity to meet others of like mind. These may include people whose brains you can pick or who represent other networking opportunities that are career enhancing in some way.

Some routes, such as a course in, say, a language, may be wholly relevant if that is something you need. Consider two overall categories first:

- *Technical:* a plethora of technical degrees and qualifications may be relevant for you depending upon the field in which you work. They may range from engineering to topics of much greater complexity.

- *Business:* these also include a wide range of things, from the now ubiquitous MBA to specialist degrees and diplomas with a more direct link to particular functional areas: sales, marketing, management, IT, human resources and so on.

Both categories are too wide to go into here, but whether you want to obtain a postgraduate MBA or a qualification linked more specifically to a business function (often professional bodies are the place to investigate this) there may be some checking out to be done.

Continuing professional development

This links closely with qualifications. In the last 10 years or so the concept of continuing professional development has spread widely in response to the kind of changes going on in the world and the increased need for professionalism in many jobs. Initially limited to the professions (areas such as accountancy and law), CPD, as it is referred to, is now a regular feature of many peoples' lives.

Definition: essentially, CPD is a programme of ongoing development undertaken as a mandatory part of someone's membership of a professional group. Activity is specified in broad detail, a set amount of time must be dedicated to it and records kept of exactly what has been done.

The requirements of professional bodies apart, such a scheme provides both added discipline to foster a commitment to ongoing self-development and a mechanism to create the necessary continuity. Of course, what is done must be selected to make it genuinely useful (not just to clock up the necessary number of CPD points), but if that is the case then such schemes are very valuable.

Some people are involved by virtue of their speciality. For example, some people will automatically be part of such a scheme (for example, that run by the Institute of Chartered Accountants); others will opt to be involved (for example, by registering to be a Chartered Marketer as part of their membership of the Chartered Institute of Marketing).

A final point: after much talk of careers, an additional point is worth making – sometimes several careers in fact run in parallel. I am referring here to what is called a *portfolio career*. This is a term for working in a way that allows you to do more than one thing. It is predominantly used in the context of those who are self-employed or in small businesses (for example, I operate in training and consultancy as well as writing books and articles), but is increasingly possible in larger organizations as well; indeed it may be a useful first step to a career change. The wider the scope of what you do, or will do in the future, the greater becomes the number of areas that development must address.

So, career development, and specifically getting career fit, must be on your mind regularly; don't let times when all is going well – for the moment – blind you to the need for it. It must also be a regular part of your activity, as thinking about it is not enough. Both individual actions and/or the continuum of what you do can jump you ahead, particularly when linked to an awareness of opportunities and a considered view of what you see as constituting career progress and success.

> **!** **ACTION:** There is potentially much to be done here, and such things can be easy to put aside 'for later'; some thinking, identification of desirable action and then resolve (which means making lists, deciding timing and keeping track) can pay dividends.

The final chapter sets some priorities.

9

Summary: 10 Steps to Being 'Career Fit'

He who would leap high must take a long run.
— Traditional (Danish) proverb

Everything touched on in this book essentially comes back to one thing. Given that you work, and are likely to go on working, in a dynamic environment you have to actively plan and take action to stay secure and move ahead. The word development, both in its general sense, and in its 'training' sense, sums up what the task is here; and yes, it is a task. As Alvin Toffler, the futurologist, said, 'The illiterate of the twenty-first century will not be those that cannot read and write, but those who cannot learn, unlearn and relearn.'

That said, remember that development, while the initiative for some of it may come from the organization, ultimately stands or falls on what *you* do. Therefore the attitude you take to it, and the action you take, dictate whether or not it will help you perform as you wish and achieve what you want now and in the future. The following does not attempt to repeat what has been said elsewhere, or even necessarily be comprehensive, rather it encapsulates under a neat 10 headings the key things that can help you make a success of what you do in development.

1. Resolve to be a regular 'self-developer'

This may seem an obvious starting point, indeed it is. Most people would agree that development is a 'good thing'. In surveys about job satisfaction people regularly rate the fact that they want to be learning and moving forward in terms of their capabilities as a prime requirement of a satisfying job (and, as has been said, the same sentiment is also applied to managers – *I want to work for someone whom I learn from*). So far so good: development is desirable and to be taken advantage of wherever possible. But this is not sufficient.

As has been made clear throughout the previous text, just taking up opportunities for development is not enough. Taking them up unthinkingly or without considering the development possibilities inherent in them is worse. For example, how many appraisals take place in organizations every day that are no more than going through the motions? They are neither constructive nor likely to lead positively to improved performance in the future. How many of these would be more useful if more thinking and preparation was done?

This is just one example (albeit an important one; witness the space given to appraisals here), but it makes a point – you need to take an initiative with development, both with activities on offer, in order to get the best from them, and certainly with the self-development activity that you plan and implement personally. Doing so must become literally a lifelong habit if you are not to short-change the process of career building or let matters go by default.

2. Analyse and set clear objectives

This needs a mention and is rightly high on this list of 10 key areas promoting career success. The details (set out earlier) will not be repeated here. Suffice to say that given pressure of time, and perhaps money too, you must have a clear focus for all your career-development activity and a clear direction to aim in, too.

Without this, time can be wasted doing things that, although generally sensible, do not address your specific development objectives sufficiently accurately to be as useful as alternative action. One of the first business maxims ever to become a well-known phrase was a saying already mentioned – *if you don't know where you are going, any road will do* (the late Peter Drucker). It makes as much sense for an individual as for a business.

3. Make and use a plan

Plan the work and work the plan, so says the old adage. It is true, it is common sense; yet it is easy to overlook and to regard planning as a chore. A programme of self-development first needs some analysis and clear objectives. A plan – which means having something in writing – is actually a time-saving device. It ensures that things are not overlooked, that each activity can be made to relate sensibly to all others and allows necessary fine-tuning along the way.

A plan should not be a straightjacket. It is more akin to a route map that allows you to plan an unfamiliar journey – yet also helps if things do not go to plan, for instance allowing rerouting to avoid road works or accident. The description 'rolling plan' makes sense here. This is something that is clear in the short term, perhaps specifying 100 per cent what you intend to do, and which sets out a clear idea of the time beyond – to be filled in progressively as time goes by in the light of actual circumstances.

The rule is simple: make a plan and put it in writing. The extent of it is actually less important. I know people who plan their career development scrupulously in this way and what results is a folder with just a few, perhaps only half a dozen, sheets of paper (or a file in a computer that they view on screen), although it can, of course, link to other things. It need not be onerous to create, or voluminous in extent; it is a foundation to what you subsequently do and very valuable in making things happen.

4. Create sufficient time

In the modern workplace there never seems to be time for anything. Pressure, stress, meetings, administration, travel and traffic and more (not least people: colleagues, customers, the boss – whoever) all conspire to keep us on the run. Setting priorities clearly is a must. If you do not concentrate on the things that matter most, then you will never get the results that you want.

Every job is different and has its own priorities. Most of these are linked to actions geared to producing the results you are charged with achieving. But there are other priorities, too, and development is certainly one of them. We are all familiar with the maxim to work smarter, not harder. It is a valid comment. You need to see development, and particularly self-development, where you have to find the time yourself, as a means to an end. It is an investment. Time spent now helps make what you do in future more effective; it directly links to the results that you want to achieve. It also links to longer term aims, in that you may never gain the advancement you want if you are constantly failing to fit in actions that would constitute firm stepping stones along the way.

In some organizations development is specifically targeted in time terms. In the financial services area, for example, this is typical, with many members of staff having to spend a set number of hours per year simply to keep their 'product knowledge' up to date in what is a heavily regulated industry. So, it will help if you:

- set yourself some sort of target;

- address separately the things you do entirely at your own behest, and those that management initiates and thus allows time for (even if you have help to ensure that the initiative takes place);

- develop and stick with appropriate habits so that some of your self-development becomes a useful routine (for example, dwelling on the lessons stemming from making a single presentation for a moment afterwards, if making good presentations is a definite career skill for you).

Time management is made effective largely through many details, there sadly being no magic formula that automatically produces excellent productivity (see *Successful Time Management*, Patrick Forsyth, Kogan Page); making sure that you do not short change your development intentions is key to your success.

5. Learn from experience

As the old proverb tells us: experience is the best teacher. Certainly it is true to say that at the core of self-development, separate from any methods, systems and processes, is one key thing – you. The attitude you take, and the way in which you harness your experience so that it provides a basis for change and better opportunities for the future, is vital. You can make a real difference.

Looking at your own job you need a sound understanding of the way it works and what makes it successful, then you have a reference against which to view your own practice and experience. Doing so must become a habit. You need to:

■ Be conscious of what you do, literally task by task, day by day.

■ Consider – analyse if you like – how particular things worked; for instance looking at how you handled a particular project, management meeting or presentation.

■ Record areas of note. These may be things that went well that you want to repeat and build on or things that could be better and need consideration, experiment or change.

■ Act on this process, adjusting your future approaches to take lessons into account.

Realistically, of course, you are not going to indulge in lengthy contemplation after every hour of the day, but if you can get into the habit of pausing regularly to consider then this is literally invaluable. A similar approach can be brought to bear on every aspect of your job, asking yourself questions such as: Was that course attendance (or appraisal or meeting) useful, how did I play it and are there ways in which I can make the next such experience work better?

Make experience work for you, effectively accelerate it and you have regular, pertinent learning on tap on an ongoing basis. This strengthens the effect of every other aspect of development to which you are exposed.

6. Learn from others

Your career progress is sufficiently important to leave no stone unturned in looking for ways of giving it strength. There is no monopoly on knowledge or ability, so you need to be in touch with others who can act as a catalyst to your development process. They can help ensure that you maximize what you achieve and make it easier to do – and perhaps more fun – at the same time. Like so much else this needs some systematic action; it is not simply a matter of tapping any useful people you happen to know. You need to:

- Identify those people both inside the organization and out that might be able to help you (these include colleagues, management in functions such as HR, people doing similar jobs elsewhere).

- Make and maintain contact, have meetings, exchange e-mails and generally keep in contact on an ongoing basis.

- Recognize that such networking must be two-way to be self-sustaining, in other words other people must find their contact with you as useful as yours with them is – give as well as take.

- Link ideas, suggestions and experience gained this way with other activities to maximize its effectiveness; for example use a particular contact as a sounding board to help prepare a contribution you have planned for a forthcoming meeting or project.

Interesting and valuable alliances are possible. Sometimes it can start with a particular swap: you want to pick brains on one subject and are able to help someone else with advice in another area. Ultimately this overlaps with the idea of mentoring (which was explored in Chapter 8).

7. Spot opportunities

There is a difference implied here between recognizing opportunities, by which I mean you should see and take advantage of ongoing processes and events such as your regular job appraisal, and spotting what one might call ad hoc opportunities. Something like a scheduled appraisal is difficult not to notice. The distinction makes the point that some opportunities are less obvious. Some things are unpredictable and you need the habit of being alert to any possibility that might assist your development and career plans.

Linked to the idea of keeping an eye out for opportunities should be that of experiment. As just one example, I have sat on various committees over the years and an immediate reaction is that it is not my favourite thing. However, it is something that is, on occasion, worth trying (you can always say that you will attend a few times before committing yourself more permanently) and I can think of more than one spell on committees that started somewhat reluctantly but from which I learnt a great deal and met people who were of further assistance.

This is another principle that needs consciously adhering to in the light of a busy life leaving no room to observe or explore anything but the most obvious.

8. Utilize a mix of methods

There is more to heart surgery than reading a good book. So too with forging your career: you need to come at it in a number of different ways. First, recognize that there are two paths to development that you can influence:

▪ Taking advantage of things 'in place' – from getting the most help from your manager to making appraisals a constructive process; here *self*-development adds to a process that would do something anyway and makes sure you obtain maximum benefit.

very easy to form clear intentions, take some action but allow an initial lack of success and the ongoing pressure of work to let you sideline them and do little or nothing more. Sustaining a programme of career- and self-development needs some commitment and some persistence.

If you aim high you may still not achieve the peak of success, but you are more likely to achieve more than you would with lower intentions. There are four manifestations of this:

- *Excellence:* in terms of everything you do and the professionalism with which you do it you should aim for excellence. Getting by is not enough; unless you are ahead of the game, unless you are constantly moving forward you are vulnerable to changing circumstances and what you do may no longer impress people as it should. In a dynamic environment the status quo is an enemy; as Henry Kaiser said: 'You can't sit on the lid of progress. If you do, you will be blown to pieces.'

- *Challenge:* you should not rule things out too readily as being beyond you. Only by accepting a challenge do you have the chance to make progress, and in any case more job satisfaction comes from taking on and making a success of something genuinely challenging than from just 'ticking over' and allowing a job to become repetitive.

- *Advancement:* this applies to success in your current job and to success in terms of your longer term career also. If you fail to take the necessary early steps then you may effectively block your progress and regret it later. It may seem like a heck of a jump to sales director or managing director, but each step on the way may well prove – or be able to be made – manageable.

- *Skills and techniques:* to do a particular job you need to be able to do, and do well, the things that it necessitates. So you need to take on the challenge of developing new skills, perhaps especially those of whatever job you see as your next step. Such things often seem daunting. There was a stage in my career when the last thing I ever thought that I would do, or wanted to do or indeed thought I would be able to do, was public speaking. I hated the very idea. But circumstances led me towards it. I had to learn how to do it – and have in fact spent a major part of my subsequent career in training involving speaking to groups of all sizes; and indeed teaching others so to do. Again you must not rule out areas of development for the wrong reasons; and these include just having distaste for them, or having a lack of confidence in your ability to do them. Aiming high includes embracing the acquisition of all the skills that will take you where you want to go.

Certainly, all this demands a positive attitude; see Chapter 2. So, be positive about your work and your ability to meet expectations. Be positive about your ability to succeed and make progress: do the right things in the right way and your chances of success, and the level of success you can achieve, increase.

Afterword

Success is not the result of spontaneous combustion.
You must first set yourself on fire.
— Fred Shero

As this book has made clear, you need to work at becoming and remaining career fit and do so in a considered and systematic way. Success does not just happen, but you can make it happen and doing so acts to forge success, achieve specific objectives and make disaster less likely. Your attitude to and action regarding career building is a key part of what allows you to do this. Not only will this approach serve you well in good, or everyday times, it will protect you in bad times. The last chapter highlighted some of the most important approaches and principles. Let's end with a few more brief dictates:

- *Look the part:* in whatever way is appropriate; you are best to go for the high end of the prevailing style in your workplace with regard to dress, for instance. Here, incidentally, I always reckon it is more difficult for women than men to make the right decision; men have a more limited choice. Remember too that appearance is much more than just how you look; what about your desk, office and more? Your manner contributes here, too.

■ *Manage your time effectively:* success demands good productivity and good time management is a skill you can acquire. Allied to this, you should deal with any stress rather than accept it and struggle with it.

■ *Behave:* the workplace can (should?) be fun and there are occasions when you can let your hair down (the department may go out for riotous drinks in celebration of business or personal achievement). However, do not let this get out of hand. You do not want the wrong kind of reputation and there are hazards, such as drink, that can quickly dilute your professional image. Most bosses would rather promote the office cat than someone with even a hint of a drink problem. Similarly do not be typecast as a rumour monger, a time waster or as possessing any other unsuitable characteristic.

■ *Don't burn your bridges:* this is a difficult one. There are issues that should be tackled (say bullying in the workplace), but move heaven and earth to do so informally first if you want to retain your career fitness. It may not be right, but realistically you are not going to be seen as the asset you once were after dragging your employer through an industrial tribunal, nor will it necessarily enhance your CV.

■ *Cut your losses:* sometimes the best tactic is to walk away. An employer, or boss, that is just so difficult that they hamper your success may be changeable, but it usually pays to decide sooner rather than later if they cannot be changed – and make a change yourself. You do not want to spend a long, difficult period that ends with you feeling you should have moved on earlier; doing so affects your job satisfaction and your building experience, and a sterile period does your record no good.

■ *Be ready for emergencies:* even the most career fit person can be caught out sometimes (just think, banks used to be regarded as safe places to work). If you have to move on, it helps to be ready to do so.

■ *Achieve:* don't take your eye off the ball, remember that a significant part of what makes you attractive to an employer is your ability to achieve your targeted results, whatever they may be; so work and career development may need to march in parallel, but priorities are important.

■ *Check rewards and satisfaction:* there is a balance here and most people do not really want to maximize reward but lose all satisfaction. At the same time, especially after a while with one employer, it is easy to find you are being taken for granted and under-rewarded.

Remember the old saying, originally attributed to Vidal Sassoon, and still worth noting: *The only place where success comes before work is in the dictionary.* True enough; the trick is to recognize the fact and work at it, but also to make the necessary work as painless as possible. Well-chosen career development activity needs exactly this approach. Thereafter it is how you proceed next that matters. Remember what Kahil Gibran said: 'A little knowledge that *acts* is worth infinitely more than much knowledge that is idle.' You may never be able to say that you are guaranteed a lifetime of satisfactory employment, but by constant career management and development you may be able to guarantee maintaining lifetime employability and achieving most, if not all, of your ambitions. The same approaches may also see you avoiding disaster or surviving it better if it does strike.

Although care and consideration is always sensible, you may also sometimes need to stick your neck out and take a chance (I would certainly never have enjoyed more than 20 years of self-employment without doing that). Opportunities, even when successfully spotted, are not always within arm's reach; sorry I'm mixing my metaphors now.

> **!** **ACTION:** In a dynamic and unpredictable world success is still well worth striving for. It can be hard work, as Lord Thomson of Fleet said, 'If one wants to be successful, one must think. One must think until it hurts. One must worry a problem in one's mind until it seems there cannot be another aspect of it that hasn't been considered.' It is all too easy to allow things to go by default. Indeed I have heard a saying to the effect that a diary is something in which we aim to write one thing, but all too often must write something else. Plan what you want to do and plan, too, to take the necessary steps along the way.

Forging a consistently successful career, maximizing its success and making sure it allows you to achieve your ambitions and draw satisfaction from it, is manifestly not a matter of good luck, so I will not end by wishing you good luck (although a little of that certainly helps). But I wish you well with it. Success is, after all, down to you, but it is possible; go for it and who knows? You may surprise yourself.